D0375004

THE VIEW FROM THE VYSOTKA

ALSO BY ANNE NIVAT

*Chienne de Guerre: A Woman Reporter Behind the
Lines of War in Chechnya*

ANNE NIVAT

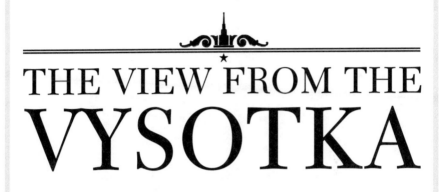

THE VIEW FROM THE
VYSOTKA

A Portrait of Russia Today
Through One of Moscow's Most Famous Addresses

Translated from the French by
Frances E. Forte

St. Martin's Press **∞** *New York*

DK593
N5813
2004

THE VIEW FROM THE VYSOTKA. Copyright © 2002 by Librairie Arthème Fayard. Translation copyright © 2004 by Frances E. Forte. All rights reserved. Printed in the United States of America. No part of this book may be used or reproduced in any manner whatsoever without written permission except in the case of brief quotations embodied in critical articles or reviews. For information, address St. Martin's Press, 175 Fifth Avenue, New York, N.Y. 10010.

www.stmartins.com

"The Cockroaches," by Yevgeny Yevtushenko, is reprinted courtesy of the author. Translation copyright © 2003 by Donald Fanger.

Library of Congress Cataloging-in-Publication Data

Nivat, Anne.
    [Maison haute. English]
    The view from the Vysotka: a portrait of Russia today through one of Moscow's most famous addresses / Anne Nivat; translated from the French by Frances E. Forte.—1st U.S. ed.
        p.   cm.
    ISBN 0-312-32278-X
    1. Moscow (Russia)—Biography. 2. Moscow (Russia)—Intellectual life—20th century. 3. Post-communism—Russia (Federation) I. Title.

DK593.N5813 2004
947'.31086—dc22

                                                                2003058691

First published in France under the title *La maison haute: Des Russes d'aujourd'hui* by Librairie Arthème Fayard.

First U.S. Edition: February 2004

10   9   8   7   6   5   4   3   2   1

CONTENTS

PART THREE: RENOVATIONS

PREFACE

Russia—the very word conjures up both staggering size and unfathomable mystery. "What's it like there now?" people ask when they learn that I live in Moscow.

As a journalist, it is my job to provide clear, concise answers to big, complex questions. As an unabashed Russophile, it's my hope to share my knowledge and my love of this fascinating and perplexing country. But how to do that? And then I found the answer—right where I live.

In the center of Moscow sits a microcosm of twentieth-century Russia in the form of a building, mostly a residential apartment complex, though there are commercial establishments on the ground floor. This building has been an epicenter of political, cultural, and social life in Russia for fifty years. From the time it was built, on Stalin's orders, the building has epitomized all that was great and all that was horrible about the twentieth-century Soviet Union.

In March 1918, Vladimir Lenin, head of the new Soviet Socialist Republic of Russia, decided to transfer his government from Saint Petersburg to Moscow, away from the encroaching menaces of World War I. Having been bypassed for centuries, the medieval city was headed for major modernization.

Yet it wasn't until 1935 that a "General Plan for the Reconstruction of Moscow" was proposed by Lenin's successor,
Joseph Stalin. This plan was both functional (wide roads with
underground crosswalks, permitting rapid evacuation in case
of attack) and ceremonial (for parades). It retained the config-
uration of a central ring intersected by radiating arteries, the
ancient design of the city.

Stalin's projects were nothing if not grandiose. The old
commercial quarters surrounding the Kremlin were razed,
avenues widened by fifty feet. Gorky Street—the principal axis
road, formerly used by imperial processions and still the main
artery from the prestigious northern suburbs, now called by its
pre-Soviet name, Tverskaya—was judged too narrow. Behind
the historic houses along its length, officials erected much
higher new apartment buildings, then removed the inhabitants
from the old houses and dynamited them.

Thus began the radical transformation of Moscow from the
seat of an ancient aristocracy into a modern city—tall, proud,
and socialist. "Nearly the entire history of Soviet architecture is
that of diverse attempts to transform everything at once from a
19th century city to a new socialist capital," notes journalist Alexi
Tarkhanov in his book *Moscow, Third Rome, Stalin's Capital.*

Gigantic work sites sprang up everywhere. The first subway train rumbled out in May 1935, which was also the year
five stars, symbols of the socialist state, were mounted on top
of the Kremlin towers. Hundreds of churches were demolished. In the center of Moscow, the imposing Cathedral of
Christ Savior was, at first, spared. It had been built on the site
of an ancient convent in the second half of the nineteenth
century to celebrate the victory over Napoléon. But eventually

it, too, was demolished so that a work of towering ambition and symbolic significance could occupy this prime real estate—the Palace of Soviets.

For such a special project, the Bolshevik government held a "democratic" international competition, in which world-famous architects Le Corbusier and Walter Gropius were among the entrants. The Italian entry was modeled on the Colosseum and the Tower of Pisa; the Germans were inspired by the Art Deco styles in vogue in the 1930s. First prize was awarded to an American project that was evocative of the White House. Events resumed their more predictable course when, having been awarded a "Special Jury Prize," the design by Soviet citizen Boris Yofane was designated as the one that would be used.

The propaganda machine went into high gear. "A grand work to be the symbol of the Stalinist epoch will be constructed in the capital of the Soviets, the Palace of Soviets," one newsreel of the time trumpeted. "It is a monument to the glory of the genius of the Revolution created by Vladimir Ilyich Lenin. It will be one thousand, three hundred, and forty-five feet high: three hundred and seventy-five feet higher than the Eiffel Tower! Even the one hundredth floor of the Empire State Building will be one hundred and seven feet lower! This accomplishment will amaze the population of the Soviet Union." The same newsreel went on to say that "an imposing statue of Lenin, about one hundred and sixty to two hundred and forty-five feet tall, will be mounted on the edifice. It will be twice as high as the famous Statue of Liberty at the entrance to the port of New York. The arms of Lenin extended above Moscow will be ninety-eight feet long."

A call went out to the finest architects, engineers, artisans, and sculptors to work out the details and bring this formidable dream into reality. In 1940, heavy construction commenced. An immense basin was dug into the former site of the Christ Savior church, and foundations of reinforced concrete were set in place. When World War II started, the steel in the framework of girders was needed for military production. The work site was deserted. Furthermore, it turned out that the geological study that had been done was inaccurate; the basin was constantly filling with groundwater.

Although the Palace of Soviets was never finished, its awe-inspiring silhouette formed the basic model for seven spectacular skyscrapers that did become reality. They came to be called *vysotkii,* an abridged form of the Russian word for multistoried buildings, *vysotonoy zkany*—literally translated as "high houses." Stalin's idea was to use these monuments to Russian socialism as weapons of anti-American propaganda. Journals of that time published descriptions of Manhattan by Maxim Gorky and Vladimir Mayakovski, who had seen only ugliness in the famous skyscrapers of New York. "From afar," Gorky wrote in *V Amerike* (1951), "the city resembles an enormous threatening jaw full of ragged black teeth. It exhales clouds of smoke into the sky and wheezes like a glutton suffering from obesity."

And in "Mayakovsky ob Amerike—ocherki—stikhi" (1949), Mayakovski teased:

> Well, and the American . . .
> also has his . . .
> something to be proud of.
> He's conned the world with his New York.

Folks have been to see it.
A hundred wretched stories
block the sky.
Stories—floors—and roofs:
That's all. That's it.

Architectural "anarchy" reigned in capitalist countries, the populist Russian press harangued. In the Soviet Union, an organic line was meticulously maintained between the audacious and innovative style of these seven monumental edifices and Moscow's historic properties. For example, the vysotka's pointed formations were tapered in order to blend with the multitiered churches and clocks of the Kremlin and the well-preserved Novodevitchy monastery.

Propagandist rhetoric was on full display in the July 1949 issue of the *Organ of Soviet Deputies and Workers of Moscow:* "These grandiose works carry us high into the light and the winds to meet the sun and the sky. Their splendid monumental shapes are triumphant symbols of the liberated work of men in our fortunate country." But it was the correlation between Soviet modernism and the styles of the past that was most emphasized in *The Skyscrapers of Moscow* by N. Kulechov and A. Pozdniev (1954): "Optimism, realism, joy of life and harmony find their expression in the silhouette of these edifices, in their colors and in the details of their decoration. Many of the stylistic elements were derived from the classical models of Russian national architecture. The massive lower sections of the structures are whittled down in proportion to their remoteness from the height, and finished off by the little round pointed towers in four sections, the spires, the coat of arms, the stars."

Thus Moscow was to be remodeled, but in a way that harmonized with the history of the nation. The seven identical skyscrapers were geographically situated both to mark the path of future expansion of the city and delineate its natural boundaries. Two were built along the Moscow River, two on the belt of gardens in its center, and another adjacent to the gardens. A sixth vysotka dominates the Ploschad trekh vokzalov (Plaza of three stations), terminals for trains to and from the entire country. The last vysotka became the University of Moscow and was perched high on a hill southwest of the center, like an enormous fortress overlooking the city.

The structures were to be flamboyant pyramids of stone, masterpieces of the Stalinist empire style, and towering icons of ideology. Each was to have its own restaurants, garages, hair salons, pharmacies, shops, a movie theater, plazas, and terraces. The vysotkas reflect the fundamental dialectic of Stalinism— halfway between the spiritual and the functional, the despotic and the populist.

The first of the giants was built in the Taganka neighborhood, east of the Kremlin and just across the river from it. (Today, when foreign television reporters deliver news from Moscow with a panoramic view of the Kremlin in the background, they are standing in Taganka.) Three recipients of the Stalin Prize worked on this project: A. Rostovsky, M. Gokhman, and Dimitry Chechulin, who in 1947 had been entrusted with the task of preserving the picturesque characteristics of the capital, reconstruction of the radial arteries, the green spaces of the grand plazas, Hotel Russia, and the White House. In Sergey Krivonos's documentary film (Quadrat Film, 2001) about the vysotka, Yuri Dykovitchny, one of the builders, claims the project was closely supervised by the Ministry of the Interior: "To construct the skyscraper, one needed access to the manpower of prisoners. They were organized in brigades, each under the direction of an engineer (nondetainee) employed under contract. These engineers who directed the work gangs had the rank of colonel in the Ministry of the Interior."

The building was erected where the Yauza tributary empties into the Moscow River, an ancient quarter where guilds of boilermakers, potters, blacksmiths, and others established themselves during the Middle Ages. The topography is picturesque. Behind the building is a sloping mound of earth that, until the eighteenth century, was called the Mount of Lice, which was probably a distortion of its earlier name, the Hill of Pungent Herbs. Even today, the door of a building facing the Taganka trolleybus stop carries this name. Both rivers wind around the front and sides of the structure. The embankment bordering the facade on the Yauza is called Podgorskaya ("nearby hill"); that which extends along the Moscow River and during the period of the Moscow reconstruction was enlarged and covered with asphalt is called Kotelnicheskaya ("ironmongers workplace").

The complicated blueprint took the shape of an elongated letter M. The right section—now called Wing A—under construction from 1940 to 1945, extends the length of the Kotelnicheskaya embankment. The left section—currently known as wings V and VK—was added in 1953 and borders Podgorskaya. These two sections form the two legs of this elongated M. The entire structure was designed to hold about eight hundred apartments and became home to almost 3,500 people. The overall ground surface of the skyscraper is 270,000 square feet, of which 160,000 is habitable.

The center of the vysotka—Sector B—fans open like a huge book toward the Kremlin to the west (the inner angle of the *M*) and rises to a height of 570 feet. Three short branches of twenty-two floors each, extending from the left, right, and middle axis of the central core, enclose the area behind it. The median section is surmounted by a hexagonal tower of seven tiers. Above that is a nine-sided tower of smaller diameter, which in turn extends into a 125-foot-tall spire. At the very top was a five-pointed star, resting on a wreath of laurel leaves.

Red granite covers the outer walls of the first four floors of the central facade; all other surfaces are gold-toned bricks. The multilevel arrangement of the ensemble of buildings is emphasized by sculptures, etchings, and architectural orna-ments. "In spite of its heavy walls," read a 1953 article in *Soviet Woman* magazine, "the house seems light and airy. Its openwork silhouette appears to have been sculpted in ivory." Four high-vaulted porticos permit access from the quays, forming a courtyard filled with greenery. Trees climbing the terraced hills obstruct the view of garages that were con-structed in the 1950s for 200 cars, a rarity in those times. Twenty high-speed elevators, another unusual amenity, were brought back from a defeated Germany as "reparations."

The central lobby is grandiose, as we can see in this contem-porary description from a 1954 edition of *The Worker of Moscow*.

> Never again will such stone steps and front entrance doors of
> their equal be constructed. They are worthy of a palace. The
> granite steps, the columns and glazed glass doors, these
> are only the beginning of the splendor that accompanies

the resident all the way to his apartment. Passing over the threshold of the principal entrance, one finds oneself in the main hall. This hexagonal space, as well as four others similarly situated in the other entranceways, emphasizes the uniqueness of the edifice. Spots of light gaily play on the white marble walls of the twenty-five-foot-high hall. The luster of hundreds of luminescent lamps is reflected in the polished red granite floor. Breadth, space and richness of decor are the sort of accommodations that such a room offers.

The rare criticisms published at the time were to be found only in the specialized architectural reviews. Primarily they point out that the exterior architecture was so elaborate that it did not harmonize with the interior architecture of the buildings. "The very large quantity of diverse, raised elements interrupts the unity of the building and divides the silhouette into parcels," read a review in *Architecture of the USSR* in 1952. The article also criticized the design of the upper level: "The spire does not seem to be truly proportional to the tower, nor to the architectural elements which surround it." The sharpest criticism concerns the immense vestibules that, "with their authoritative and cold architecture," "lack warmth and intimacy" and resemble "the vestibules of prestigious public facilities."

But the beneficiaries of this place were amazed by its immensity and elegance. Who were these lucky tenants?

Shortly before the building was ready for occupancy in 1952, there was a fuss over the rumor that the list of future residents proposed by Lavrenty Beria, the legendarily infamous Commissioner of the People at the Interior Ministry, had first been examined by Stalin personally. Noting that the names were·not of people he knew, Stalin was supposed to have declared to his right-hand man, "Tell me then, besides these people, *nobody* else lives in Moscow?" The lists were immediately revised and the apartments granted to the most prominent people in Soviet society.

Thus the original occupants of the Taganka skyscraper were not average renters. They were the Soviet intelligentsia—writers, composers, artists, film directors, and actors known throughout the country, as well as high-level bureaucrats from the Ministry of the Interior and the security services and military officers of the highest ranks. "It's thanks to Stalin that we owe the presence here of [Bolshoi ballerina] Galina Ulanova and [writer] Konstantin Paustovsky," the magazine *Itogui* observed ironically in its article titled "Order of Installation" on August 7, 2001.

With these men and women, or their descendants, I passed many hours in the conversations that make up this book. Each of them has a special rapport with this building, where many have spent all or most of their lives. They make the building a living museum. Slave labor built this Communist "workers' paradise." Interestingly, some dissidents lived behind its luxurious granite and marble walls. So did KGB agents, spies, informers, and their victims. The supposedly nonexistent upper class lived here. Today some of the new Russian elite, those who have found success in the open market economy, have also chosen to live here, whether in spite of or because of the building's history.

Since I moved here in 2000, this building has spoken to me—through its architectural concept, its construction details, its hardworking staff, and, most of all, its residents. My neighbors personify the full length of Russia's geographical, political, social, and historical spectrum. Some are prospering, some are just coping, and others are struggling, either against the "new Russia" or to hang on desperately as it passes them by. Both native and foreign perspectives can be found in this magnificent edifice. Here are the witnesses to the past and the leaders of the future. Here is the answer to the question with which I started.

Like the country it symbolizes, this vysotka is a hulking presence, a nearly overpowering mishmash of architectural vernaculars combined in a structure of astonishing breadth and visual impact. So unique is its style that the word vysotka has come to be associated only with the seven specific structures in this same style in Moscow.

Anyone in the market for Moscow real estate today knows that you want a Stalin-era building. On one hand, pre-Revolutionary structures have nice high ceilings and thick walls, but they also have all kinds of plumbing, heating, and electrical problems because they were built before such utilities were available. On the other hand, buildings from Khruschev's era were built by "happy citizens of the workers' paradise" and are dangerously shoddy, to the point of tilting ominously and visibly crumbling. Stalin used political prisoners to do the hard labor on his buildings; they nonetheless have structural integrity and reliable wiring. He may have been a murderous tyrant, but he was good for property values.

The vysotka in Taganka—my vysotka—has been officially classified as a historic landmark and is finally being preserved. In this book, it is the people living there, my neighbors, whom I mean to preserve, for their lives and times represent the wider experience of Russia during the last half-century. During

Stalin's time, the crème de la crème of Russian society were invited to live here, and those people and their descendants still constitute a large percentage of the residents. Today they are among the poorest residents.

Many of the people I talked to were simply given their apartments; in the Soviet Union, permission for any citizen to reside in an apartment was granted by the state, which owned all the property. Private housing was a special privilege, and many joined the Communist Party purely in order to get higher priority in housing allocations. People were told when and where to move, sometimes after spending years on waiting lists while crammed into squalid communal living situations (*kommunalka*) in which an entire family might live in one room and share a single kitchen and bathroom with many other families.

The housing shortage could lead to awkward social situations. It was common for married children to live with their parents and for divorced spouses to continue to live together, in one room, even with new spouses. Most Russian couples only had one child due to lack of space. Even today, Russian real estate is described by the number of rooms an apartment has (not including the kitchen and bathroom)—for example, a "two-room" or a "four-room." The number of bedrooms is never stated; it is still assumed that all rooms will serve multiple purposes.

The real estate market being, officially speaking, nonexistent, the only way to leave housing that had been granted to you by the state was to find an "exchange," i.e., a person (or family) who agreed to come live in your room or apartment while yielding his or her own apartment or room to you.

Barters were based on estimated values; money very often passed under the table.

When the occupant of an apartment died, the right to live there passed to whichever member of the family was properly registered at that address at the time. If no one was, the apartment reverted automatically to the state, which in any case had never ceased to be the owner. Registration was and remains an extremely important aspect of life in Russia, as you will see. Residents are still registered at an address and given an official stamped document called a *propiska*. Moscow *propiskas* are highly valued because there are many more jobs there than in other parts of Russia. Even visitors to Moscow must register their address within three days of entering the country.

There was no such thing as property ownership, as we understand it, until the early nineties. Today many apartments have been privatized as part of the first post-Communist economic reforms introduced in 1991 by eager ultraliberal economists, who intended to transform Russia as quickly as possible into a market economy—a policy called "shock therapy." Through a simple administrative maneuver, millions of tenants of government apartments were able to become the owners of their lodgings, and for ridiculously low prices. Privatization gave people the right to sell or rent out their apartments, even to bequeath them to their descendants.

Nevertheless, by 2001 only 44 percent of apartments in Moscow had been privatized this way. The reason is that by privatizing a tenant loses his place on the waiting lists for government-subsidized housing. Apartments continue to be allocated practically free of charge to certain of the either best-connected or most seriously underprivileged citizens. The wait is still ten to fifteen years. For many older citizens, unable to make a living in the new market economy, dependency on the state is preferable to property ownership. Horror stories abound of people who sold their apartments for what seemed like a lot of money but couldn't find another place to buy for the same price because of the rampant inflation, caused in large part by the privatizations.

Even those who have the money to buy a private apartment in Moscow today still live with the social consequences of Communism. The aging infrastructure means that every year, sometime between May and August, every apartment in Moscow will be without hot water for a few weeks while maintenance is performed on pipes and boilers. During frigid winters, most Moscow residents wear light clothing indoors and sleep with windows open because of overheating and the absence of individual furnaces or thermostats. (However, in many areas outside Moscow, people are often without heat when ancient boilers and generators break down and freeze before they can be repaired.) Almost every apartment I've ever seen has an armored outer door and multiple locks. Steel bars are standard on windows of the first three floors. Robbery was a problem under Communism, too. And Russian apartments have also been the targets of terrorism. In 1999, three Moscow apartment buildings were blown up at dawn and over 300 residents were killed, allegedly by Islamic terrorists from Chechnya associated with Al Qaeda.

Another consequence of "shock therapy" occurred when some state-owned industries were transformed into public stock companies, literally overnight. Former Communist Party bosses and other political insiders managed to control most of the stock without paying for it, resulting in the wholesale plunder of the most valuable assets in the country. This robber baron phase has now matured into an industrial oligarchy that controls most of the Russian economy, including the media and the election process.

Increasingly, educated young people have established businesses that thrive in the absence of commercial laws, and an extremely wealthy entrepreneurial class has made Russia the number one market for both Mercedes-Benzes and murders-for-hire. People who have been able to take advantage of the new politics and economics are called the new Russians. You'll hear that expression a lot in this book, as you would hear it often if you lived in Russia.

Some of the people in this book mention the "thaw" that took place during the Khruschev and Brezhnev administrations in the sixties and the late seventies, when some of the social limitations were eased. But they more often refer to the "financial crisis of '98," which occurred after Boris Yeltsin ordered the devaluation of the ruble in August of 1998. Personal savings evaporated overnight and foreign investors fled. While Americans were obsessed with news about Monica Lewinsky, Russians were experiencing a crisis from which they are only now beginning to recover.

How do the Russians of today live? What do they dream of? What do they regret? What are they afraid of? I will let the residents of my vysotka provide some answers. Some of the residents are very famous, others unknown. Taken together, however, their testimonies sketch a picture of life in Russia under dictatorship, under Communism, and under democracy. At a time when our perception of Vladimir Putin's Russia

remains hazy, I will focus upon the ambiguities of contemporary Russian society, rooted in the complexity of human relations under Communism and still adjusting itself in these first
years thereafter.

What better way to know what it's like to live in Moscow
than to look inside the windows of literally one of Moscow's
most storied addresses?

ANNE NIVAT

Moscow
August 2003

PART ONE

THE ELEGANT GIANT

CHAPTER 1

Push hard on the heavy, glazed glass outer door. It swings open dramatically, narrowly missing a buttress. You're in a small unadorned vestibule that traps the frigid outside air and provides a brush mat to scrape muddy ice off your boots. Turn to the right (access to the left is temporarily blocked) and pass through two more high doors, which also resist. Here, finally, is the cavernous main lobby—the domain of the building attendants.

Zoya and Lida sit authoritatively behind a wobbly table, lists of the residents and their telephone numbers close at hand, as well as an orange plastic Soviet-era radio. Various envelopes are arranged neatly before the women. Against the adjacent wall is a large worn-out divan, also orange, an incongruous presence in this immense and solemn hall.

"Lida Nikolayevna knows the names of all the children in the building. Me, I'm satisfied with the names of the dogs," jokes Zoya.

"That's because there are a lot fewer children than dogs," Lida clarifies, amused. She is petite and pretty, even at sixty-five years old. Her hair is pulled up in a perfectly coiffed chignon, but her knit pullover is a bit out of style.

3

"It dates back to the Soviet Union," she says apologetically. She's the sort of person who takes great care with all her tasks. With her spectacles, Zoya has the air of a strict grandmother. These two women team up to work a twenty-four-hour shift. There are eight building attendants in all in the Taganka vysotka, one man and seven women, of whom three live in the building.

The main lobby is the command center of the building. Through the partly open door of the dispatching department a lot of technical equipment can be seen. Someone monitors it continuously.

"That's the computer," explains a housekeeper in the process of dusting the hall.

The tall silhouette of a soldier wearing a camouflage uniform and leather boots appears in the hall. He shoots a quick glance and makes a barely perceptible nod at Zoya and Lida, sitting at the attendants' table. They know him. Though doing his military service, he also performs odd jobs for one of the residents. He is allowed to proceed toward the elevator without stopping, as is normally required.

The staff meeting in the dispatching center ends at around eleven o'clock. Today Nina Andreevna, seventy, is one of the housekeepers who clean the elevators. During the heyday of the new skyscraper, she served as a uniformed elevator operator. She used to sit on a jump seat and press the floor number buttons, a function that has not existed since the elevators were automated. Today's meeting has made her nervous.

"I'm seeing a computer for the first time in my life," she tells her two colleagues and friends. "No, no, not a computer with games, a computer that does everything on the keyboard that we used to do manually on the control panel. Well, it seemed to be very simple. They showed us what to push on, and how to make the mouse work! We're giving it a try anyway. I am as tired as an Olympic champion after the race."

She sets herself down behind the attendants' table.

"Are you familiar with these new gadgets? If I forget to press on a button, the computer tells me . . . or rather, it writes to me—on the screen! Now that's progress."

She crumples and squeezes hard on the dust rag lying in her lap.

Seventy-five-year-old Zinaida Leontievna, the second elevator attendant, also hangs around to chat after the same computer training session. Her face has a defeated expression.

"I don't understand how that thing works. I'm going to have to quit this job. I just can't do it."

Lida gasps. Zinaida is one of the pillars of this vysotka, having worked in the skyscraper since it first opened fifty years ago. She greets everyone by their first name and patronym, their father's given name, the customary and respectful mode of address in Russian. This house is these women's universe. Zinaida even lodged in dormitories reserved for technical service personnel for forty-eight years, until she was finally granted her own two-room apartment in a low-rent suburban apartment building two years ago. A woman of small stature and round face, with large, coarse hands that handle the broom skillfully, Zinaida sweeps the floor day and night. She has carelessly pulled on a long smock, which is a bit bunched up over woolen hose. Her gray hair is cut straight and held back by a headband. The only vanity that she allows herself is a pair of earrings. Freckles are scattered across her drab face, brightened up by sparkling large blue-gray eyes. This morning, however, they have lost their twinkle. On the verge of tears, she casts a tender look at the old-fashioned instrument panel, with orderly levers and switches of white and red, which she will no longer be using.

The nostalgic reverie is broken when a young woman strides past them and toward the elevators at a determined pace. Lida and Zoya shout together: "Hey there, young lady! Which apartment are you going to?"

The young woman stops in her tracks, turns, and tells them. Lida pounces on the orange telephone to announce the visitor, who waits for permission to proceed.

By noontime, nothing is left on the hall table except copies of the *Times of Eurasia,* a publication of the Eurasian Party of Russia, a somewhat mysterious sociopolitical organization of emigrants from Central Asia. The bulletins are spread out like cookies and offered free of charge. Two young Caucasian-looking men arrive to present an invitation marked: "Hand Deliver in Person." It is addressed to the actress Klara Luchko. People from the Caucusus Mountains in the Muslim regions south of Russia are often discriminated against in Moscow and all the Christian, European areas of Russia, in part because of their darker skin and Muslim religion and terrorist activities related to their fight for independence from Russia. Lida decides not to let them wander around the residential floors and calls the actress to inform her that some messengers have arrived. The line is busy. Lida suggests that the two men wait on the orange divan. They will be allowed to go upstairs a little later.

Lida takes her tea break in a kitchenette off the entranceway.

"I wish I could close my eyes and open them to find we have returned to the Soviet Union. All countries have bad features. In the USSR we had to line up for everything, that's true, but the food wasn't so expensive!"

She sighs. After working for forty years, she has had to become a concierge here in order to survive. When can she hope to retire? The sad fact is that she has no one to count on but herself.

"Here contact with people is pleasant enough," she says.

Still, making the commute once every four days between Ironmongers Quay and her suburban apartment is very difficult. She would have much preferred to continue working at her previous employer, Gosstandard, a government bureaucracy in charge of certifying technical standards, where she spent thirty years. From the sixteen floors of the office tower this agency used to occupy, they're down to only one. The rest were rented by commercial firms at fair market prices.

"If only we had taken the best parts of the West, instead of choosing the worst!"

While Lida savors her cup of tea with toast and jam, Zoya brings some cookies just given to her by a resident.

There are fewer comings and goings now. The telephone is silent. An elderly resident joins the attendants, settling herself on one of the four chairs around their table. She removes two ten-ruble notes (worth about thirty-five cents each) from her pocket and gives them to Lida "for the month of February." Although the residents pay thirty rubles (about one dollar) per month for monitoring of the building, they also give an additional tip.

"Only twenty rubles, and she didn't give anything in

January," Lida complains after the old lady leaves. "Even though her daughter is in Germany, she could still pay more!"

Twenty-three-year-old Natasha passes by. She pauses for a moment to chat with Zoya and Lida. A first cousin of Julia, wife of the singer-songwriter Willy Tokarev, whom we will meet later, Natasha recently arrived from Krasnoyarsk, in Siberia, to look for work in the capital. She is a bookkeeper by training and has been working as the building's chief dispatcher since yesterday, keeping track of the maintenance staff as they handle repairs and scheduling tasks. The new computer doesn't intimidate her.

"So far, I don't know my way around the city at all, so I need to get used to it. I am here to make enough money to pay for the education of my younger brother, who wants to practice judo at a professional level. He seems to have the talent," she explains timidly. "In Krasnoyarsk, it is very difficult to find work, and even so, I would earn much less than here."

An unknown woman approaches them, lugging a bulky sack on wheels. One by one, she begins to remove women's tailored suits made of wool and cotton from her voluminous bag and spreads them out for display on the attendants' table. She's a Russian who chose to live in Riga (Latvia) when her husband, an ex–Soviet soldier formerly based in Estonia, found himself without work after the independence of that republic in 1991.

"Find me customers, please," she implores.

Her prices are fairly high: 2,500 rubles (about eighty-five dollars) for a suit, at least a thousand rubles more than Zoya's and Lida's monthly salary. Nevertheless, Lida cannot restrain herself from holding one of the skirts up against her waist. It's much too short, though the real problem is that Lida cannot afford it. Zoya, however, seems genuinely tempted.

Late in the afternoon, Sofia Perovskaya, president of the Owners' Association, informs the ladies that around 8:00 P.M. there will be a meeting of about fifty garage owners in the Veterans' Conference Room. Tenants or not, the attendees will have to pass before the professional scrutiny of Zoya and Lida.

Just as that gathering is getting started, the actor Anatoly Borisovich returns from a concert.

"May I use your telephone for a moment?" he asks them timidly.

Zoya and Lida know he cannot make some calls from his apartment because his wife watches him so closely. Lida is used to his asking, which happens frequently.

"I pity Anatoly Borisovich. His wife is really nasty." Lida lets him make his call.

Florian Fenner, a German man who lives on the ninth floor, arrives with a box of Swiss chocolates in his hand and offers it to the delighted guardians.

"Are they really better than Russian chocolates?" Lida asks, opening the box to find out for herself.

An American resident stops by to warn the ladies that he will be hosting a party in his apartment this evening. He hopes that his guests will be allowed to pass through. He massacres the Russian language and has difficulty understanding Lida and Zoya's reply that there will not be any problem. Lida is amused by his grammatical stumbles.

A messenger girl delivers an envelope and sits down to gossip for a moment. Lida asks what her monthly salary is for this kind of work.

"One hundred dollars," she responds. Lida's face assumes a dreamy look.

Zoya has already gone to lie down in the small sleeping quarters near their workstation. Following their arrangement, she rests from 10:00 P.M. to 3:00 A.M.; then she takes over from Lida. The woman from Riga comes back, carrying suits under her arms.

Zoya wakes up. She pulls out a pair of dressy shoes and the key to the Concorde Room, formerly an elegant ballroom, now used for meetings and special functions. Equipped with a mirror, it will serve as a dressing room. Lida stays at her post, though she is dying to watch Zoya try on her first suit.

A few minutes later, Zoya steps out a new woman. The dark blue skirt fits as if custom-made for her, and although her white collar is frayed, she still looks rather elegant. She faces Lida and waits for her opinion.

Lida is speechless, which Zoya takes as a compliment. She really wants this outfit, which becomes her more than it would the others. Would the lady from Riga let her borrow the blue suit so she could show it to her husband?

"Yes, yes, I'll come back tomorrow." She's sure of a sale.

Just then, a tenant and her twenty-two-year-old daughter pass by. A second opinion! They huddle together in front of the mirror. In spite of the late hour and public setting, the central concourse has been transformed into a boutique atmosphere.

Lida goes back to her lonely night watch.

CHAPTER 2

She is one of the vysotka's veterans, queen of the old comrades. In a bulky green pullover sweater and matching rabbit fur hat, which she is never without, Sofia Perovskaya, former engineer, is the great-grandniece and namesake of a member of the revolutionary committee that made the decision to assassinate Czar Alexander III and was executed for it. She recalls the words of her father, who, until the advent of perestroika, had occupied the post of vice president of Gosplan of the "Soviet Socialist Federal Republic of Russia," as she still makes a point of calling it. Under Communist Party guidance, the state planning committee, Gosplan (acronym for Gosudarstvennyy Planovy Komitet), was primarily responsible for creating and monitoring the Soviet Union's economic plans.

"He always repeated: First the social need, then the private interests. Today's leaders of Russia have long since tossed this slogan into the trash heap."

Sofia Perovskaya, still a dedicated Communist, remains faithful to those principles.

In 2000, Sofia was elected president of the Owners' Association of the building. Each entryway (*podyezd*) to a particular wing or section of the building (*korpus*), which together

11

with the others form a housing unit (*dom*), elects its own representatives, who have been meeting once a year since 1996. The association is the successor of the former Soviet *domkom* (house committee), which in turn derived from the traditional pre-Soviet *samupravleny* (committee of self-management). Today every condominium or cooperative apartment building has some kind of association.

The *domkom* was especially active in the fifties. It took care of child care, decorated the communal areas with flowers, and organized social activities. Life back then was simpler, according to Perovskaya: "Everyone knew what to do and what it was worth, and everyone was responsible for his actions." As soon as a technical problem arose, the dispatcher called the electrician on duty, who sent someone to fix it. The repair was done free of charge. Every month the building superintendents verified that everything was in good working order, that the faucets were not dripping, that the elevators were functioning properly. Every year the electrical system was gone over with a fine-tooth comb. According to Sofia, maintenance started to degrade as soon as the "democrats" took power, after Mikhail Gorbachev imposed his perestroika. She spits out the word "perestroika."

Officially the Taganka vysotka remains city property, municipal housing that falls under the auspices of "Directive Number 15 of Skyscrapers of the City of Moscow," the civil administration that oversees the seven skyscrapers built under Stalin. Directive 15 assigns a director for each building. He or she is responsible for the work crews, electricians, plumbers, elevator operators, housekeepers, and dispatchers, as well as the clerks in the passport office and the accountants who administer the budget. The entire staff (about 150 people) therefore consists of municipal employees specializing in the maintenance of the elegant giant. The Owners' Association, however, is independent from the management of the building and from the municipal bureaucracy. During their annual meetings, problems are discussed and proposed solutions submitted to the director.

One of the major problems is the need for renovation. On this point, the Taganka vysotka's Owners' Association, in the person of its president, has been highly effective.

"Since the mayor of Moscow, Yuri Luzhkov, does not allocate us enough money to renovate this immense structure, I considered it my job to pull the alarm bell and take the matter all the way to the Duma," explains Sofia Perovskaya, referring to the Russian parliament. She seemed both irritated and very proud.

"In our house, everything is made worse in proportion to the general degradation in the rest of the country. But thank God we are always here to monitor the situation. There is no question of us letting things go, and, in the final count, we are relatively better off here than elsewhere."

The gigantic job of renovation began in Wing A, the oldest part of the skyscraper, in 1985.

"It was a matter of replacing the ductwork and wiring in every apartment, but there wasn't enough money. The projects slowed down; then they stopped. So you could say that the skyscraper remains almost exactly as it was when it was placed in service fifty years ago."

Two arguments seemed to have convinced the city finally to take action in the matter of renovation. First, the year 2002 was the fiftieth anniversary of the skyscraper; and second, the Taganka vysotka, as well as the one located on Barrikadnaya Square, is unique in Moscow and even in Europe. The five other Stalinist skyscrapers are not residences like those in Taganka and Barrikadnaya but, in whole or in part, administrative office buildings or hotels. In the end, thanks to the local Duma representative, renovation was included in the city budgets for 2000 (a little over 10 million rubles, or $325,000) and 2001 (7 million rubles, or $225,000).

"These are miserly amounts for such a gigantic building!" complains Perovskaya. "But it's better than nothing. The laborers needed access to every apartment to drill through the walls," she explains further. "Afterward the holes were refilled, but not repainted. It was a very expensive renovation, which many owners couldn't afford. As for those who had already made the repairs in their apartment, they certainly weren't pleased, and some complained to the director about it. Those people didn't realize that the skyscraper belonged to the city!"

Apart from the headaches of renovations, Sofia Perovskaya's other big complaint is about privatization.

"The paradox of privatization is that it gives the residents the impression that the premises belong to them. But no, not so at all. We are not really owners, except of the air between the walls! That's Luzhkov's fault." She points at his poster on the wall. "And the new real estate laws. The "shock therapy" that was applied in Russia may suit five-story buildings without elevators or incinerators, but not a monster like this. If it was up to me, all buildings more than twelve floors high should remain public property."

Eliminating restrictions on buying and selling housing property soon created the same kind of real estate market conditions that exist in the West. Consequently, two types of owners coexist in Russia: the "private" owners (those whose apartments have officially been privatized) and the hundreds of thousands of tenants of the state government who pay symbolic rent and continue to wait years, even decades, to be allocated a permanent lodging.

"This has a lot to do with the mentality of the Russian citizen," laments architect Victor Cherediego. He moved into Wing A of the skyscraper in 1950, when he was seven years old. His father, a general in the Ministry of the Interior and two-time winner of the Lenin Prize—the Soviet Union's highest civilian citation for service to the state—was granted a five-room space with a view of the Moscow River.

"My office consists of six rooms, which I bought one by one from residents of a former *kommunalka*. I tried to buy a seventh space, but the old woman who lives there refuses to leave. Even though I've offered to buy it from her at fair market value, she still refuses to sell because she is on a waiting list to receive an apartment and doesn't want to give up her place. Most socially disadvantaged people still believe that their only recourse is the state. This system of obtaining free lodgings should have been dismantled ten years ago."

Since the dissolution of the Soviet Union, all local governments have recognized that they need to buckle down and reform community services, but most haven't dared to do what it takes. One drastic measure, increasing monthly maintenance fees, is particularly unpopular. The general chaos of the first post-Soviet years forced the government to pay almost 100 percent of the communal expenses. Since then, the nonprivatized units have received lower subsidies from the struggling state governments. As a result of the lack of maintenance, today, in Moscow 60 percent of the communal infrastructures are unusable and one-third of the underground pipes and 17 percent of the sewers need to be replaced. A presidential decree in 1997 called for the population to pay 90 percent of the real costs of lodgings beginning in 2002, and the current government has proposed 100 percent individual responsibility by the end of 2003, a goal that will not be met, although the percentage paid by individuals has climbed steadily from 2 percent in 1992 to about 50 percent in 2000. Pres. Vladimir Putin has declared that Russians must pay realistic prices that conform to worldwide standards, noting that one cubic meter of gas was billed to Russian residents at one-tenth of the price in Western Europe.

Thus in Moscow, as in other regions of Russia since the beginning of the nineties, the communal expenditures (water, electricity, heat, garbage, antennae, upkeep of common areas, et cetera) have kept going up, but at the vysotka on Ironmongers Quay they have been held down to 900 rubles (about twenty-nine dollars), thanks again to the actions of Sofia Perovskaya, ever attentive to the fate of pensioners, who collect an average of only 1,500 rubles (fifty dollars) per month, and other disadvantaged occupants of the building.

Her battles are being fought on another terrain as well. Once the Federal Law on Condominiums of June 1996 permitted it, a group calling itself Skyscraper on Ironmongers Quay was set up to pressure residents to create an American-style condominium, which gives owners the right to rent or sell the common areas of the building. According to Sofia Perovskaya, who does not even bother to greet these "troublemakers" anymore, this was the act of people who lived in the building during Soviet times and who "think they can get away with anything."

"They are not necessarily rich people," she observes, "but those who want to enrich themselves on our backs after we have been thrown out. Oh yes! In fact, their goal is to rent out the open spaces of the building. Fortunately, those of us who have a head on our shoulders remain a majority."

As the *Moskovsky Komsomolets* newspaper noted when it investigated the subject in May 1995, "The new elite of the building are bourgeois, but still act like 'Chekists' [the first name of the national security force was the Cheka, predecessor to the KGB, and its agents were known as Chekists]. Several times, posters appeared in different hallways. They read: 'Advice to the residents of the building. As recently reported, the mayor of Moscow has approved our relocation. A foreign company will renovate in order to transform our building into a hotel! Let's act! The only way to prevent this madness is to take charge of our homes. Let's create a condominium!'" Frightened at the idea of finding themselves in the minority, many residents—especially elderly people unfamiliar with such matters—were persuaded to sign a petition in favor of condominium conversion.

Theoretically, if the vysotka became a condominium (which is not the case for any of the seven vysotkas), the expenditures related to its maintenance, management, and development would cease to be an obligation of the state. They would henceforth be within the jurisdiction of the Owners' Association. In

addition, the owners would have the right to construct, renovate, and resell habitable space, even to rent or sell nonlivable
spaces of the condominium structure and condo land.

The residents would therefore have the ability to transform their building into a profitable enterprise. *Moskovsky
Komsomolets* theorizes: "All the residents of the building
therefore think they have a chance of getting rich, but, in fact,
this is not the case because everyone might have to absorb a
sudden increase in maintenance fees."

With regard to Ironmongers Quay, the situation is complicated by the fact that the building is "classified." Being
"classified" means being designated as a historical structure
by Directive No. 620 of the mayor of Moscow, Yuri Luzhkov,
in March 1987. Moreover, in Moscow (where a special statute
applies), the "sale" of land actually means purchasing either a
forty-nine- or ninety-nine-year lease rather than outright
ownership. According to the most recent legislation, no sale
of land to private individuals for the construction of individual housing is authorized except in suburban zones or in the
countryside.

"In the West," Victor Cherediego emphasizes, "private
property has always existed and the owners are always invest-
ing in the maintenance of their structures. Here the horrible
gap of seventy-five years during which the state did nothing
made us unprepared to change to a new system. The true concept of property does not exist in Russia. This often perplexes
potential investors, who realize that it is better to demolish and
rebuild than to renovate."

Of the 800 apartment owners in the Taganka vysotka,
hardly 100 would have the means to sustain a condominium of

this type. Elena Andreeva, a businesswoman who lives in Wing A, is one of these. However, Sofia Perovskaya counts Elena among her allies against the condominium.

"Elena Andreeva, who bought two apartments in Wing A, which she is renovating, is a member of our Owners' Association and we are very proud of that. She undoubtedly belongs to the class of 'new Russians,' but she joins us in our fight to preserve this vysotka, because it is about a fight that started with perestroika. This house is mine, it's my fatherland, my parents lived here, and now my granddaughter is growing up here. As for me, I will die here.

"But there is also something we cannot do anything about. It's impossible to stop work from being done inside the apartments, because a municipal decree by our dear Luzhkov authorizes them between seven in the morning and eleven o'clock at night every day except Sunday! On the fifteenth floor of the central part, an American succeeded in getting all the work he wanted by bribing all sorts of authorities. So you see, our own civil servants are really responsible for this chaos! Admittedly, our vysotka is classified, so nothing prevents the management from giving authorizations instead of money, each one more foolish than the other."

Since 1953 Sofia Perovskaya has lived in a four-room space above the Illusion Cinema in Wing VK. She does not discuss her private life much but does not hide her nostalgia for the regime that disappeared in 1991: "When our friends came to visit us, they thought they were entering a museum! At that time most of them still lived in huts. People were good; everything was different. I don't understand all the criticism of those days. Everything was less expensive. You could find everything, even Italian shoes, as long as you were willing to stand in line. Our economic system started to collapse with Igor Gaidar's liberalization—'shock therapy.' The ten thousand rubles that I inherited from my father in the early nineties could have bought two cars or twenty refrigerators. The next day, with two fewer zeros [on the currency], I was left with one hundred rubles [about three dollars]! There's a reform that slit our throats! Of course, the former system was not ideal, but there is no doubt that the government was more powerful then. Stalin died eight years after the end of the war, but he had time to put everything that had been destroyed back on its feet, and the prices returned to their previous levels. Stalin also left two and a half tons of gold reserves, which disappeared under Gaidar. I wonder if we even have two hundred and fifty pounds left!"

CHAPTER 3

Larissa Nikolayevna, a good-natured fifty-two-year-old loyal Communist from a Party-affiliated family, has directed the Concorde Center for three years. After she worked her way up the ranks from provincial official to Moscow bureaucrat in the midseventies, adapting to life in the vysotka was not without difficulties at first. But her Party affiliation enabled her to integrate more quickly, and when she was asked to take part in various social activities in the building she did not hesitate. She takes the "new Russia" in stride, though she also admits that she doesn't understand it.

"In 1981, when the building manager suggested that I work as principal of the house kindergarten, I immediately agreed. I started with four hours per day. Back then we offered ten different activities, such as sewing, drawing, painting, Ping-Pong, chess, et cetera. We occupied an immense space on the twenty-fifth floor of the central tower with an amazing view. But our room opened onto a terrace, and it was difficult to prevent the children from going out there. We had to watch them constantly. What's more, the residents complained that the children didn't behave in the elevators. We ended up moving down to the ground floor.

"We reported to the management of the building until the end of the Soviet Union. Then, in 1993, we decided to reregister as an autonomous social service enterprise under the auspices of the municipality. We chose the name 'Concorde,' meaning harmony, which is so difficult to attain within this building. Our affiliation with another governmental unit protects our existence. The city counts on us, they know us, although I'm pretty sure we irritate the vysotka's management because we occupy space and don't bring in any income.

"At Concorde, all activities are officially free and open to all the children in this area, big or little. On Mondays, twenty-three kids are enrolled in drawing class (their works are displayed on the wall). On Wednesday, Thursday, and Sunday, Julia gives painting lessons, just because she enjoys it, since her husband makes enough money. Tuesday and Saturday, there's aerobics. The children have to sit still all day at school and at home, so it's good for them to move a little. In connection with this, I heard President Putin declare recently that he wished our young people did more sports. Still, it's necessary that we provide this opportunity to average citizens.

"A young woman runs the remedial teaching classes. These days, in order to enter first grade at school, the child needs to already have a certain level of knowledge. In the old days, we took the students as they were. Within a year, we had also set up a physical education course, but we needed a locker room. After much stalling, the director finally granted us a tiny space without ventilation in the cellar of the fourth entrance of Wing V. We had to abandon it.

"Finally, a chess club, very highly regarded, meets in Wing A on Saturdays and Sundays at one and six P.M. There are always lots of amateurs, but some are seriously competitive. The only problem is that the management makes us do without a telephone—which we would pay for—in order to sell the access line to a commercial firm. As a result, since I live in the same wing, it's me who receives the phone calls from anxious parents."

In the room reserved for the chess club, twenty or so old tables and wooden chairs are arranged along the walls; an upright piano donated by a resident is relegated to a corner. There is also a fax machine, a gift from the main office, that is unusable since the telephone line is no longer available. Larissa carefully guards the telephone handset, "just in case." The list of twenty-three chess players posted on the wall includes one girl.

"The instructors are paid directly by the parents. In fact, the families give whatever amount they want—there is no rule. Some pay fifty rubles [about two dollars] or more. Others, like for example unmarried mothers, cannot pay anything. There is no point to our saying anything. You can tell; you can see it in their children, how they are dressed, if they have pencils or paints to draw or paint with, et cetera. In fact, very few children from this building are registered here, simply because so few children live here. Then again, women have fewer children today.

"Before perestroika, we took advantage of the Illusion Cinema from time to time. The former director of the cinema let us go for free, but we don't know the new director. In those days, the financial situation was different, of course, and we were able to organize excursions to museums, even outside of Moscow. Today, our center is partly financed by the district, which for the year 2002, allocated twenty-five thousand rubles [$800] for our annual budget, and ten thousand [$325] for excursions. The current building manager gives nothing but a symbolic sum for New Years celebrations, which take place at the site of the *krasny ougolok*.

"Literally meaning 'small corner of honor,' the *krasny ougolok* is an ironic imitation of the 'corner of honor' in the Russian cottage, where, opposite the entry door, one traditionally placed the most beautiful icons. In the Taganka vysotka it refers to the place where Communist Party meetings and propaganda sessions used to take place. Now it's where the children decorate the fir tree and gifts are placed under it.

"This year, four artists came to entertain the children. They were paid three thousand rubles [$100]; plus the fir tree cost three hundred rubles [$10]. Fortunately, the city district offered us ten thousand rubles [$325] for gifts. Under the Communist regime, we had no trouble getting additional funds. Today, it takes courage to go beg from the director! As someone here says, coal is the master of the house, and the director claims that he has no money."

"Coal is the master of the house" means roughly the same thing as "those who control the purse strings rule." We step outside, because a pupil is about to have a lesson, and find ourselves in a mirror-lined dance studio with parquet floors. This is actually the former library of the building. It has not been used since its librarian, Serafina Ivanovna, died four years ago. Now all the books are stuffed in cupboards.

"One day we'll find somebody to replace the priceless Serafina Ivanovna, but like all volunteer jobs, it does not attract many takers. My personal retirement pension has risen to fourteen hundred rubles a month [$45], and my husband, a former soldier who is also retired, earns a bit extra working as a night security guard in a commercial firm."

Larissa is shocked to learn that in the West "to go into retirement" means to stop working altogether.

"This work helps me to find and maintain my equilibrium. It does me good to see the smiles of these children, to hear their laughter. It recharges me to be near them. And besides, if I announced my departure, I'd be afraid someone would take advantage by closing the center permanently.

"I come from Novgorod, in the north. I got married in Moscow in 1976. My husband, like his father before him, was a military man. His parents lived in a two-room space in Wing A since 1952. The first time I entered this vysotka, I felt so small! For the first four years, we rented an apartment elsewhere because my husband earned a good living. My mother-in-law was a capable woman, overflowing with energy. She handled staff policy on the personnel committee of the building. She attended their sessions every week until the eighties. The vysotka's Party organization was very influential. The Communists living here were for the most part retirees, but thanks to their connections and sophistication, they could find out anything. They knew everything. When my father-in-law died, my mother-in-law did not want to live alone, so we came back and moved in with her. She died in 1981. I think she simply could not survive perestroika. She would never have been able to understand the country's political evolution. After her death, there were four of us, me, my husband, and our two daughters. Masha, the younger, is twenty-four years old and still lives with us.

"My daughters and I have different opinions about Russia.

My elder, who works in a commercial firm, tries to persuade me that if I were young today, I would have the same lifestyle she does, totally different from the youth that I knew under the Soviet Union! She lives without schedules and when necessary can work from ten o'clock in the morning until very late at night. That was unthinkable in my time. But she earns her own living, and she likes it that way.

"It is impossible to argue with her about salaries. She earns about twenty-five thousand rubles per month [$800] and contributes most of our family budget. It's kind of her to share this money with us while she is not married. She's always after me to stop looking to the past, but nostalgia remains strong.

"Children today have a concept of what property is, and they deserve a different life from ours. My younger earns enough as a baby-sitter, enough to pay a special tutor to prepare her for entrance exams to the university. If we had a son, I wonder if he would have become a soldier like his father and grandfather. The prestige of the uniform has completely disappeared. I was proud my husband was a soldier. Maybe, when it comes to prestige, the military men have been replaced by businessmen?

"My youngest often tells me that she will not vote. I try to reason with her because I find it unthinkable not to vote. Young people have less civic awareness than us. I don't know what the future holds. In the last presidential election, in 2000, I voted for Gennady Zhuganov, the leader of the Communist Party. In 1996, I voted in the first round for Gregory Yavlinsky"—leader of the liberal Yabloko Party—"then for Zhuganov in the second round. I don't like Putin. Don't ask me why. He is the heir to Boris Yeltsin, and his election was a set-up job!"

CHAPTER 4

It's a Saturday afternoon in February. The daunting granite wall of the vysotka seems even more implacable in the icy white light. Indoors it's too hot, as is usual in most urban Russian buildings, where the centralized heat cannot be individually regulated. We take a left off the lobby and descend the steps leading into the dance studio.

In preparation for a concert and recital in honor of the Russian writer Pushkin, benches have been arranged behind the upright piano, which a young woman is playing. A portrait of Pushkin rests on an easel in full view of the audience. Brightly colored plastic flowers stick out of a wicker basket. Some elderly ladies have already arrived and are seated next to one another on the rickety chairs. Most of them are dressed up in formal clothes and look like they just came from the hairdresser—though one wears a wool cap.

From the back, the pianist, with her long blond hair and fuchsia blouse, has the awkward air of an adolescent. She is perched atop a pile of books that is balanced precariously on a chair. When she turns around and smiles, it becomes clear that she is at least seventy-five years old and is wearing a wig.

Valentina Ivanovna, seventy-eight years old, looks elegant

in her long black skirt and white blouse. With an anxious but businesslike air, she carries an armful of papers—the concert programs—and sits down as if to set a good example. She keeps saying over and over that it is time to start, that we cannot wait anymore. Suddenly she gets up and runs out into the hallway to usher in some latecomers. She tries in vain to persuade Lidia Smirnova, an elderly film actress who lives in the building and who happens to be passing near the attendants' table, to come join the festivities, to no avail.

"Our show will start now," Valentina Ivanovna finally announces to an audience of fifteen people, of whom three are men. One of them will record the performance on an antique tape recorder; another, with an imposing array of polished medals decorating his jacket, is using a handheld video recorder.

"Stop and go sit down," Valentina Ivanovna snaps at the pianist.

Removing the books on her seat one by one, the pianist yields her place to a young man in a dark suit.

Silence settles but is soon broken by Valentina Ivanovna's thin voice, which exhorts the assembly to "remember their illustrious poet" Pushkin on this 165th anniversary of his tragic passing. Then she signals to the pianist to commence. This is also the cue for a woman with frizzy hair, gold high heels, and a fringed shawl—heavily made-up—to come onstage and start reading a text about the day of the poet's death. Pushkin was fatally wounded in a duel with a military officer, Baron George D'Anthes, in January 1837.

Wearing oversize pince-nez, Valentina Ivanovna concludes the reading with the words: "Nobody in Russian can do without him." Both women then yield the stage to a man in the costume of the blue king of Tergal, a character from one of Pushkin's stories, who advances with head bowed, a dreamy expression, and a collection of Lermontov poetry in his hand. Without taking a single glance at his text, he recites, without error, motionless, his blue eyes lost in the distance. The audience applauds.

Valentina Ivanovna stands up again. She says that according to Lermontov—a great poet and contemporary of Pushkin's—"the fatal duel had all the signs of organized crime. The last three days of Pushkin's writing were very productive." She pauses to direct a latecomer toward an open bench—"the chairs are reserved for the participants"—then goes on. "Despite his debts, Pushkin always insisted that his wife wear an elegant wardrobe in good taste." The audience seems captivated.

Suddenly the woman in high heels reappears onstage, a musical score in her hand. Dozens of long necklaces dangle down almost to her waist. She must be jumping her cue, because Valentina Ivanovna shoos her off and continues with her presentation, revealing the contents of some anonymous letters Pushkin received several months before the fatal duel. To discuss the duel, she announces, "in order to better understand the technical details," that she will "call on Yuri Nikolayovich, doctor of science."

"Prepare yourself to hear dreadful things," warns the man with a grave voice before plunging into the details of the gauges, lengths, and calibers of the duelists' pistols, the trajectory of the balls, et cetera.

"Pushkin was certainly shot first, but still had the strength to pull the trigger in turn," recounted Yuri Nikolayovich, visibly moved, his voice shaking somewhat. "D'Anthes's bullet-proof jacket stopped the ball. Otherwise, Pushkin would have killed him," he declares confidently, concluding that, "it was definitely not a fair fight." Applause.

Valentina Ivanovna gets up again. She tells the audience that the news of Pushkin's wound spread rapidly and that before long tens of thousands of people massed in front of his house.

"What happened next you know already," she adds, dropping her head in dismay. She summons up a pretense of cheerfulness. "But we are not gathered here this evening to be sad. So, let's continue with our program."

A young woman in a red velvet dress positions herself beside the piano. Her dress emphasizes her paleness; her expression under nicely trimmed thick brown bangs is sharp. She opens her arms wide and sings a love song, her light soprano contrasting with her "femme fatale" physique. Sometimes her breath seems to fail her, resulting in wrong notes. When she finishes, she bows to the audience, right hand placed on her heart.

The young-looking older woman in pink has returned to the piano. Different singers follow one after another, among them Valentina Ivanovna, whose high-pitched voice turns out to be pleasant. The woman in gold heels, harnessed in her heavily jeweled necklaces, reappears with a triumphant air and chants Pushkin's poem "The Gypsies"—for which her costume has given us a foretaste. Her voice is a bit shrill. When her recitation is finished, she exits stage left, reddening like a schoolgirl under the polite applause.

But the feature attraction is an extract from *Boris Godonov*, sung and acted with liveliness and passion by the more talented members of Valentina Ivanovna's chorus. Two men appear in costume playing the czar and his servant. The man who plays the czar is an excellent baritone. He wears a long tunic and false beard and has heavily made-up eyebrows.

Finally, the singer with golden heels concludes the evening by reciting—much better than she sings—parts of *Eugene Onegin*. In the rare moments when she falters, the spectators whisper the words for her.

After the show, they all congratulate one another and go back upstairs to their own apartments. A few of the old women cordially thank Valentina Ivanovna for having offered them this semiprofessional entertainment, since none of them can afford to buy a seat at the theater or the opera.

Valentina Ivanovna is delighted. This choral society, which she still calls her brigade, was formed in 1992. She is proud that one of her members has graduated from the conservatory. Once a month, she gives a concert exclusively for the most dedicated Communists in the neighborhood.

"I get the word out in the building with posters, which I paste up myself close to the elevators. For five years, thanks to an agreement with the Concorde Center, we've been meeting here every Saturday afternoon at two for an hour," explains the lively septuagenarian.

"I've lived in two rooms in Wing A since 1946. My father worked in the NKVD"—predecessor of the KGB. "He was in charge of a regiment of border guards in Turkmenistan during the Second World War. Then he directed a department in the fight against bandits. I was born in Baku, in Azerbaijan, because my parents moved around continuously. That's why I am always in a hurry to go somewhere!

"My paternal grandfather was a peasant in the Moscow region, and my maternal grandfather was a fisherman near

Baku. When we arrived at this building, I was twenty-two years old. It didn't have gas or running water yet. It was heated with wood and coal, and we had to get water from a well in the courtyard. The Ministry of the Interior even asked us to complete the utilities in our apartment ourselves! They finally hooked up the gas a year later. We were delighted to live here, even though we had to chop wood. The boiler wasn't in service until Wing A was connected to the central section of the build-ing in 1952. That's when we 'unbuttoned our fur-lined coats,' as my father used to say.

"In our wing, there was nothing but NKVD officers, cho-sen personally by Stalin. We are pleased to have artists as neighbors now. But our wing was a good place to live. In the summertime, we left the doors of the corridor wide open to make a breeze, and dogs and cats walked freely from one apartment to another. In the central building, the occupants didn't socialize and caretakers were on duty day and night.

"Being a communist, I am not religious, but my father inculcated in me respect for the church. On Easter [most ven-erated holiday of the Russian Orthodox religion], we said 'Christos voskres' ['Christ was resurrected'] and crossed our-selves. Sometimes he even ventured into places of worship during the services. One day, in the church at Zagorsk [now renamed Sergey Possad], my father noticed that a soldier had entered without removing his cap. He forced him to take it off.

"For now, we old-timers still have a certain weight in this building, which enables us to modify redevelopment projects we don't like. We recently succeeded in getting a bus stop close to the Illusion Cinema, very helpful for those of us—the majority—who don't have our own car. We also managed to get two projects involving the vacant lot located opposite Wing V canceled. The first involved building an Armenian church there, the second a garage! Luckily we saved our courtyard. They also wanted to replace our supermarket in Wing A with a car dealership. We stopped that one, too.

"I always dreamed of becoming a professional singer, but that was right after the war. My father kept repeating that all of western Russia was in ruins, that I had a fragile voice, and that I would never win any singing contests. So I decided to continue my study of literature. But I have always sung and I still do. In 1957, I even won a contest. All my life, I have given courses on song and literature.

"I have always done volunteer work for the Party organization of the building. Before the coup against Gorbachev in 1991, I was even second in command. Until the prohibition of the Party after 1991, we numbered one hundred and thirty-two registered members. Then the figure fell to twenty-three. Today, we are no more than seventeen. I am also a member of the Owners' Association of our entryway in Wing A. Just like in the time of the Soviet Union, each entryway elects its own council member and president. Back then, there were also 'propagandists' charged with undertaking the important work of political information policy, especially before the elections, and I took part in that. Last, I am also a member of the *raikom* [ruling committee] of the Party at the district level. We have all aged, but I still get around and can be counted on to do my bit.

"I have no heir, so I decided to sign a lifetime annuity contract with the elder daughter of Larissa Nikolayevna, whom I registered in my apartment so that she would inherit it after my death. In the meantime, she pays my living expenses, my telephone bill, my electricity, plus six hundred rubles [twenty dollars] monthly. I am not the only old person in this building who has chosen this solution, ultimately quite practical.

"My mother died at the age of seventy-four, in 1972, and my father two years later, of tuberculosis, just before he turned seventy. He had taken a dim view of Khruschev's policies regarding Stalin's 'cult of personality' because Khruschev had the nerve to rehabilitate everyone Stalin denounced! For my father, who had devoted his entire life to the fight against crime, these rehabilitations were incomprehensible.

"We placed a lot of hope in Brezhnev, but nothing happened. Registered Party members were no longer pure or loyal but instead true careerists. There was also a certain excitement about Gorbachev, but so much money disappeared! And where did they get the money to seed the Gorbachev Fund? In the first presidential election, in 1991, I voted for Yeltsin because he wanted to give all the power to the Soviets, but he was just playing a trick on us! After that, I voted for Zhuganov.

"Putin—what a nightmare—I am ashamed of him! When I think about how he apologized in front of the Polish people on his recent visit there, in the name of the Russian nation! 'Excused'? For what? The Polish authorities wanted him to kneel. After we freed Kraków, saved the Poles and Poland from ruin! No matter who may conquer our Russian soil, it's all we have left."

During an official state visit to Poland in 2000, Russian president Vladimir Putin did not kneel or ask forgiveness from the Polish nation, although that's exactly what the leaders in Warsaw wanted and expected. When they didn't get it, they brought Putin to the Monument of the Polish Insurrection, which had not been included on the initial program for the ceremony. This left the lingering impression among Russians that Putin apologized.

"Before perestroika, the district committee furnished us with books, as well as a list of newspapers and magazines we could subscribe to. Our library grew to a few thousand volumes over the years. Galina Kuznetsova, whose father-in-law presides over the Veterans' Council, watches over the library these days. It's open on Wednesdays and Fridays. Serafina Ivanovna used to run the office, but when she died, nobody took over after her. We also used to have conferences on specific topics; Galina Ulanova and Nikita Bogoslovsky came to speak for free to our group. We also had space in the *krasny ougolok* at our disposal for the propagation of mass culture, like for meetings of the Party and so forth. A doctor used to give examinations once a week, and we also had the opportunity to do gymnastics in the evening. Everything was carefully organized by the house committee and by the workers' trade unions.

"How do I cope with capitalism? Well, I have no choice. However, I continue to battle against this regime and I'll keep fighting until it is defeated! In October 1993, I supported the insurgents at the Russian White House by bringing them potatoes, and I would have stuck with them!" She is referring to the so-called second coup or the "Yeltsin coup," when, in October 1993, the political confrontation between the Supreme Soviet and the new executive branch provided by the new democratic constitution had arrived at such a standoff that President Boris Yeltsin deployed tanks to force out a handful of old-line Communists who were entrenched in the Russian White House.

"I've more or less adapted now, but I will carry on in my

own way to lead the life I want. On television, they try to make us believe that it is not important, but that's brainwashing. Luckily my two televisions don't work, neither one. If I want to see a good film, I go to the Illusion Cinema. I don't need anything else!

"Recently I ran into one of my fellow graduates from the musical institute who became a policeman. We started talking about politics. He said to me, 'Of course, Valentina Ivanovna, you are on the other side.' 'But which side do you think I'm on?' I asked. 'The left, of course. You could not have moved to the right! If you had changed to the other side, you would have disappointed me. I know that you are a woman of conviction.'

"I like this skyscraper so much that I still feel nostalgia for the old days, when we all lived here together. What a degree of culture we attained! What a community we were! The most beautiful furniture in our apartments was the books. We were more than a little bit proud. Have you seen the books in the apartments of these 'new Russians'? I once owned a very rich library, including original editions of Lermontov and Pushkin, but I had to sell them. Perestroika has 'eaten' them. What else could I do?

"I have had enough of the way journalists of every shade and hue describe this building—as 'elitist,' 'special,' 'an island' of I don't know what. That has only one purpose—to make our compatriots envious and jealous. To all those who think that living in this vysotka constitutes a particular honor I say that my apartment is no different from theirs! In Wing A, we didn't install a telephone until 1952, not before. Even then, my father didn't really want it or need it. His boss and many of his colleagues lived in the same entryway. Who needed a telephone?"

CHAPTER 5

ILLUSION—the huge rusted letters hang precariously above the heavy wooden double doors, characteristic of the skyscraper on Ironmongers Quay. And yet this Illusion is not at all unreal. For nearly four decades, thousands of Soviet, then Russian, citizens have been "educated" in a hall of average dimensions and mediocre comfort (the seats are made of plastic) by being shown the great film classics from around the world.

A strident alarm bell—still used in the theaters in Moscow—signals the opening of the doors. The entrance hall is grandiose: marble floors and tall columns confer a neoclassical ambiance. When the earliest residents of this vysotka, all dignitaries and high-level functionaries, crossed the threshold of the brand-new cinema, they didn't feel as if they had left the grandeur of home. Today the Znamia Room (Flag room) is no longer the big attraction it once was. Most of the time, the immense space, intended for hosting Party functions, is vacant.

The first movie theaters that appeared in czarist Russia between 1905 and 1908 all bore the name "Illusion." After nationalization of the cinema industry by the Bolsheviks in 1920, a decree from Lenin rescinded the traditional name. In 1966, fourteen years after its inception, the room was reopened under the name Illusion Cinema. This was a time of relaxed political tensions. Every "civilized" country of the world had its own film library, and the Soviet Union would not be an exception. From then on the Illusion Cinema was open to the general public. Its mission was to show the thousands of feet of motion picture film buried in the state archives, particularly the finest Soviet and foreign films. And people came. It didn't matter that the hall chosen by the cultural apparatchiks was far from the subway and difficult to get to.

The opening took place on March 16, 1966, with a press conference. *Potemkin* was shown. The next day, it was *Broken Blossoms,* a film by the American director D. W. Griffith that came out in 1919. *Grand Illusion* would be the first French film. The artistic director of the theater was Vladimir Soloviov, a young movie critic and fan of obscure films as well as classics. Today, with a poised voice and a charming smile, Soloviov recalls his battles to create the movie theater and to fight censorship:

"For nearly a year, I was going crazy, running around everywhere. It was absolutely necessary to obtain a certain number of endorsements so that my application to open this film club could carry more weight. I decided to organize viewings in factories, then got letters of recommendation from the factory director, the trade unions, the managers of the various houses of culture, to support our request to the Central Committee.

"The deputy director of Goskino"—the state bureaucracy overseeing cinemas and filmmaking—"knew the cinema well and supported our effort, because our goal was to show a different film every day. He personally signed off on the programs that I brought to him, which avoided my having to go to the censorship bureau. After a year and a half, I addressed the censor directly, whom he knew and admired. He thought highly of us. In fact, we had almost gone back to self-censorship, because in the list that I presented to them I excluded films I knew they considered pro-fascist or pro-American. Those were different times. The Taganka Theater had just opened not far from here, the journal *Novy Mir* [New World] had published Solzhenitsyn, but nobody knew the history of cinema. Our old films represented, in a remarkably artistic way, an expression of goodness, humanism, honor, sincerity, honesty, order, and of the absence of lies. When the end of Stalinism came, we educated the public.

"Illusion became a fashionable place as soon as it opened. This room offered everyone a breath of fresh air at the lowest point of the Stalinist times. Illusion was to cinema what *Novy Mir* was to literature and the *Literary Gazette* was to literary journalism. Advertising wasn't necessary—word of mouth sufficed."

"We snuck in by the back door and watched films through the keyhole," acknowledges Katya Demurova, a forty-five-year-old painter who has lived in the vysotka all her life. The evening before the first day of the month, when monthly passes went on sale, a long line formed along the quay. Some even slept in front of the cashier's window so that they would be first in line the following day. Each union had a quota of seats. In the second year of its existence, every Thursday from seven until late at night Illusion presented a series of conferences on the history of the cinema. Film students competed to attend it. Some classics like Ernst Lubitsch's *Ninotchka,* starring Greta Garbo, remained censored. But over time, ideological pressure weakened. By the middle of the eighties, they were almost ready to show work by the subversive filmmaker Andrei Tarkovsky—but not quite."

Soloviev affirms, "In 1964, the Soviet Union didn't yet have any idea about 'new wave' cinema. We didn't show either Godard or Truffaut, whose works weren't shown until our first French retrospective, organized with the assistance of the French Embassy and the French Film Club. Over the first five years of our existence, we made a point of organizing two or three retrospectives per year. A retrospective of Polish films in 1966 allowed us to offer the public the masterpieces by Andrzej Wajda, which had been banned for ideological reasons. In 1967, during our Italian retrospective, we showed Fellini's *La Dolce Vita,* which had been released in Italy in 1959. We also premiered the second part of the film *Ivan the Terrible,* a picture shot by Eisenstein in 1945. The first part of the film had received the Stalin Prize in 1946, but this second part had greatly displeased Stalin, who had noticed similarities between Ivan and himself.

"Not only were we on very good terms with journalists, we also had the opportunity to host the best film directors from around the world. Here's the book in which we saved testimonies of these visits."

He shows me a large golden notebook filled with yellowing pages. It reads like a who's who of European filmmaking in the mid–twentieth century. "We wish you all the best," was inscribed by Reuben Mamoulian, a director who made films with Greta Garbo and Marlene Dietrich. "Vive the friendship of French and Soviet screenwriters, vive the friendship of our people, vive socialism, vive communism!" wrote Pascal Aubier. Soloviov claims to have more than ten of these notebooks.

"Sometimes the films caused scandals. After an Italian progressive newspaper characterized our club as 'opposition cinema,' I was summoned to appear before the authorities. However, much bigger scandals took place much later, such as when we showed Soviet films like those of Andrei Tarkovsky. The premiere of *Andrei Roublev* had to be postponed the day before it was scheduled to be shown. I received a phone call ordering me to cancel it. But since the disappearance of censorship, we can show anything, like, for example, Leni Riefenstahl's *Triumph of the Will*, released in 1936, which was accused of supporting fascists."

"We were all a team of simultaneous translators. I was in charge of English," Gregory Libergal tells me. Libergal worked at the Illusion from shortly after its opening until the end of the eighties.

"So it was in this room that the first and best team of simultaneous interpreters in the country was formed. We sat in front of a microphone in the prompter's box. Even if we had a chance to view the film ahead of time, we really didn't know the text. We had to be careful not to speak too loud or too soft. The important thing was to get the timing right. The spectator had to both comprehend the language of the film and forget the presence of the interpreter. I watched and translated *Casablanca, Gone with the Wind,* and *Citizen Kane* about a thousand times each."

In the nineties, the television channels added films to their programming and there were VCRs in almost every home, so the general attendance at movie theaters has significantly decreased. The Illusion Cinema has continued to show old

Soviet films because all the foreign classics have already been shown. Today it is still the only place in Moscow—besides the Museum of the Cinema—where you can review or study the work of Tarkovsky and Eisenstein. The theater has not been renovated because the state subsidies are almost gone.

"But what good would it do to equip the Illusion with a Dolby sound system," Soloviev wonders, "when *Grand Illusion* or any of the other great classics in their repertoire weren't shot in Dolby?"

Today, the cinematic archives of the state, on which this cinema depends, contain more than 60,000 original film prints, not counting the copies, compared to some 50,000 when the cinema opened.

"Our objective is that in a three-year period a conscientious viewer can see all the classics of worldwide and Soviet cinema," Soloviov explains further. "Unfortunately, nothing is released in its original version anymore. Foreign-language films have to be dubbed or else the public complains. Our audience has certainly shrunk in the last few years, but no international film club in the world is well attended these days. We have also stopped giving lectures before the evening show because the interest in this kind of thing seems to have disappeared. Nobody believes what they're told anymore. They don't want to hear someone speaking from the stage."

True to its reputation, the Illusion continues to offer three shows per day, at prices defying all competition. The first show, in the early afternoon, costs ten rubles (about thirty-five cents), the second thirty rubles (one dollar), and the evening show fifty rubles ($1.70), whereas tickets for the downtown movie theaters cost 200 rubles (seven dollars). Rental space in the city costs an enormous amount, according to Soloviov, even at his preferential rate. As for the rest of the available space in the capital, there is a huge temptation for commercial firms to acquire a theater with the intention of transforming it into a restaurant or casino.

In the imposing lobby of the Illusion, a private café—in Russia this essentially means a restaurant—replete with billiard tables opens every day from noon until eleven. Five years ago it replaced a Soviet-style cafeteria that served only bottled seltzer and stale sandwiches. Today the ubiquitous "Kiev croquettes" figure on the café's menu, along with a wide assortment of liqueurs, cognacs, whiskies, rums, and martinis, which young Russians are wild about. The rental of this space brings in a little extra income to the cinema.

Old black-and-white photographs of Soviet actors are lined up along the wall beside more recent ones of Gérard Depardieu, Sandrine Bonnair, Bulle Ogier, and Jacques Rivette—no doubt donated by the French Cultural Center, which is located nearby. Portraits of legendary European filmmakers such as Andrzej Wajda, Marcel Carné, Jean Renoir, René Clair, and Luchino Visconti are also on display, as well as of some of the Russian stars who live in the vysotka, such as Marina Ladynina, who stopped acting in films almost fifty years ago. They are still popular, according to Soloviov. "The public never stops loving its old actors," he says.

"Entering into the elevator of this building," Gregory Lebergal remembers, "one felt so small. A heavy atmosphere still reigns here, even though the sixties were rather liberal."

I ask whether the movie stars who live in the vysotka really served the political regime of their day.

"It was a dilemma for the artist under a totalitarian regime," he replies. "In France, Edith Piaf—should she have sung or not during the German occupation? Everyone rationalized his relationship to the regime."

CHAPTER 6

WINGS A, V, AND VK:
THE SHOPS

Most of the commercial establishments in the *vystoka* on Iron-mongers Quay have remained as they were when they first opened in 1952. The post office and telegraph station, savings bank, bakery, fruit and vegetable stand, and supermarket are still in the same place. However, the hairdressing salon has modernized and become an imitation-Western "beauty center." And two years ago, the legendary uniform tailor shop called Sewing Workshop Number One had to lease most of its space to a discount furniture store.

Interestingly, all these businesses are run by women, either private owners or managers. They are young (between thirty-five and fifty years old) and dynamic, know what they want and have succeeded at getting it in a Russia that is still openly chauvinist and where there are few places for women in management. The second point common to these small businesses is that, when they renovated their spaces they took pains to conserve their original look—the interior decor, organization of the showcases, and choice of signage all reflect the vysotka's Stalinist roots. In Moscow, capital of extremes, where two systems exist side by side—the old Communist one and the new capitalist society—Stalinist architecture, symbolizing strength and stability, is once again in vogue.

The gigantic Sewing Workshop Number One, which originally occupied 5,400 square feet in Wing A, was the very best in the capital. The dismemberment of the Soviet empire in 1991, contributing to the disastrous state in which the former Soviet army finds itself today, had inevitable effects. Reconverted long ago into "civilian" production, the factory is now crammed into two rooms that look like a run-down pawnshop.

Nina Vassilyevna, her brown hair upswept, a tape measure slung over her shoulder, and looking very elegant in her tailored purple suit, has worked here for twenty years. She introduces me to two "old-timers" sitting behind a counter in the fitting room. One of them, Natasha Pavlovna, retains a youthful air. She has worked at Sewing Workshop Number One since 1954.

"They sent us to a training course in this workshop after our primary school education, and I stayed on here. I was fifteen years old and very glad to have found work. After a one-year trial period, I was officially hired. There were two shifts, day and night, three hundred and sixty people in all. We collapsed under the workload. We sewed shirts for men and blouses for women—of silk, wool, linen, any type of material. And then, of course, the uniforms. The customers chose their fabric on-site. We offered an enormous selection. Four teams specialized in coats for women and five in uniform jackets for men. I would receive my work plan for the day in the mornings. I teamed up with a cutter. The customers came in to have their measurements taken. Then came a series of fittings, three at most. Officially, we worked exclusively for the military command, but we always worked in parallel for their wives, and more and more often for a civilian clientele. Lots of women made a point of dressing elegantly in spite of the meager choices offered in the stores at that time. So, they frequented the very highly regarded Workshop Number One—ours!"

Natasha Pavlovna, looking somewhat ill at ease, claims to be unaware of who lived in the building back in those days. Her colleague Oksana Titovna takes the initiative to affirm that although they didn't know exactly what the NKVD was, they carried out its orders without question.

Today they have much less work to do. Last year they lost one of their clients, a military academy, probably because it found their prices prohibitive. At the end of 2000, the Russian government's decision to reduce military manpower immediately lowered sales. Entire battalions stopped ordering custom-fitted uniforms. The majority now wear simple camouflage outfits.

To make up for all the lost business, the director came up with the idea of converting the workshop into a theater costume manufacturer. Now Workshop Number One is the only place in Moscow that provides replicas of historical uniforms such as those used in musical comedies or in the films. And some occupants of the building, including the singer Ludmilla Zykina, the actor Anatoly Chirvindt and his wife, and Lidia Smirnova still number among their clients.

"If we are still here, there is no doubt that destiny wanted it so," Natasha Pavlovna resumes. "There are difficult moments, because we don't have enough manpower to do much work."

She admits now that "the folks who live here lived like kings" and that they knew that *zeks*—political prisoners—constructed this building.

"They were behind barbed wire. We went to see them during their rest break, and they made signs to us. We smiled at them; sometimes they even passed us messages. Basically, we were young and carefree, but we were proud to work here and all our friends envied us.

"Also, we are very disappointed when we don't get enough credit for our work. Recently we did a lot of work for the fashion designer Yudachkin's latest collection, but he 'forgot' to mention our workshop. It's incredible!

"We should have retired eight years ago, but we really cannot do otherwise."

Nadejda Gavrilovna, seventy-three years old, has been with the workshop for fifty years and received a medal in recognition of her seniority. Even now, with her face skillfully made-up, with midlength red-tinted hair, and wearing a leopard blouse, she gives the impression that she must have been a very beautiful young woman.

"I learned my trade in this workshop. At first I specialized in women's coats. Then, in 1959, I became a cutter, and ever since, I cut, cut, cut!" She laughs coquettishly.

"All the generals, prosecutors, and other high-level Soviet functionaries passed through my hands. Sometimes, in the summer, we played soccer and volleyball in the courtyard between two fittings for clients living in the apartments on the upper floors. This building always reminded me of a palace, of an impregnable fortress. Never, even in my dreams, could I ever have lived here. I was lodged in a *kommunalka* in the center of the city until I finally received a two-room in the suburbs. Over the years, they have offered many times to transfer me to another workshop where I would undoubtedly be better-paid. I always refuse. It feels like I was born here. Why should I go somewhere else? My monthly salary is two thousand rubles [sixty-seven dollars]. I really like to dance, and sometimes we used to dance here in the workshop during the grand Party festivities."

In another wing of the vysotka, the one that faces the Yauza River, Raissa Borissovna, age forty, reigns over the beauty center situated in the former hairdressing salon where generations of the privileged had their hair done. A doctor by training, specializing in plastic surgery, she has directed the center since 1995. They offer permanent makeup, laser depilation, and classic cosmetology, "using French techniques," as their leaflet proclaims. At the end of each day, the broad pavement along the quay becomes crowded with limousines and SUV's with tinted windows—belonging to her customers.

Raissa expresses herself with circumspection. She claims to have spent many months renovating this 3,200-square-foot space that was, when she took it over, "in a state of unspeakable filth.

"We were among the first in Moscow to use foreign technology. That was at the beginning of privatization," she explains with pride. "Today, there are several hundred of these modern beauty salons, because their popularity was immediate. I finished my studies in 1991. My goal was to go into medical cosmetology. I opened my first center in 1993. Our predecessors couldn't afford to stay in business. They were operating at a loss. In ten years, I progressed from traditional beauty care to physiotherapeutic cosmetology.

"This skyscraper is old and its plumbing is antique. It should be entirely revamped, but that requires so many discussions with the proper authorities."

This is as far as she will go on that subject. She turns away my questions about privatization: "You came to collect information about my profession? Fine, but I have nothing to say about anything else."

In any case, when she became owner of this salon, she took advantage of a 1,200-square-foot basement, which will soon be renovated to provide an employee lounge and storage closets.

"I chose this Stalinist skyscraper because it is a classy building. To come and be treated in a prestigious house constitutes a perk for our clientele, because the atmosphere here is unique. However, maintaining a business here is complicated enough. The building is difficult to get to. The state does everything it can to dissuade the small and midsize entrepreneurs from conducting their trade profitably. During the financial crisis in 1998, I even thought about giving up. Still, if I were to do it over again I would do everything exactly the same, because it is my life's work. My husband is an economist. He invested a lot of money in this business. It's thanks to him that I have been able to realize this dream. The disadvantage is that I'm here from morning until night, including Saturdays. It is the only way to satisfy my patients [she does not want to call them clients], who represent the active segment of the Russian population. I have more and more male clients, whom I must not disappoint. So every year I offer new services to remain competitive, even though classic cosmetology is still the service most in demand.

"The majority of the inhabitants of this old building cannot afford to come here, because they are mostly retirees.
However, we have selected ten elderly residents, especially
underprivileged, and we cut their hair free of charge. Other
residents of the skyscraper, like the actresses Lidia Smirnova
and Klara Luchko, the singer Ludmilla Zykina, and Nina Grigoryevna, the manager of the [Ironmongers] Gastronome
supermarket, are regular customers."

At the corner of the same wing, not far from the Illusion Cinema, is the bakery that for five decades has been the pride of
this vysotka. Since it opened, the store has never either experienced an interruption of service or changed its sign. Today seventeen women work here.

After having managed a supermarket in a district outside
the city center, Natasha Vassilyevna, thirty-nine, has been in
charge for the last three years.

"I agreed to work in this bakery not because I needed the
money but because this place always made me dream," she con-
fesses. "In my family, we never wanted for anything. My father
was a military officer. This store was never like the others. During my childhood, crossing this threshold after pushing open
that heavy wooden door, I always had the feeling of entering a
lavish palace. Never would I have thought that one day I would
run it!

"Nevertheless, it was a shock when I looked behind the
scenes of this bakery that I had loved so much. The place had
become a sort of dump, black with dirt; the magnificent chandeliers were broken. It has continually changed hands since the
early nineties, the usual distribution networks were modified,

most of the managers disappeared without a trace, and the store was running at a loss. The new owner quickly convinced me to take the position of manager. Ever since, it is a daily party, along with an enormous amount of work. Besides, fortunately, my children are grown up, because with a 'baby' like this, I would not have time to spend with them!

"I attempted to re-create the festive atmosphere that I always used to feel when I came through this door. That's why I decided to renovate everything, but in the old style, using the exact image that I had in my memory as a model. We intentionally reproduced the original interior as well, just like the exterior. I tried to recover as much as possible of the old decor. I also had the torchères made from photographs. I am particularly proud of the result."

Reddening, Natasha Vassilyevna reveals a drawer full of sketches for windows and signage:

"I always knew about sweets. The nuances between the different tarts and cakes were no secret to me. My mother worked all her life as a laborer at Krasny Oktyabr [Red October factory], one of the best manufacturers of confectioneries in the country. She passed along her knowledge and love of this craft to me.

"Since I've been managing this store it has become profitable. We had to diversify a little bit by offering, for example, a range of alcoholic beverages and delicatessen meats, but the sweets are still what we're known for. I personally selected the best of what is offered by our twenty vendors. All of our tarts are good, because I chose them from my heart." She poses her right hand on her left breast and bursts out laughing. "I love my work enormously." Her beaming silhouette confirms it.

Natasha Vassilyevna details each type of candy with a live-liness that she can't suppress.

"For me, the priority is what my heart tells me about the quality of the product that I have decided to sell, and that explains their price. Most of our production is still by hand. That shows, doesn't it? But we also sell less expensive candies, which are excellent. Some customers trek all the way across Moscow to buy a tart from us. They have complete confidence in me. Who can ask for more than that?"

Return to Wing A. Bordering the embankment that faces the Moscow River stretches the supermarket called Ironmongers Gastronome. Open until very late at night every day, including Sundays, the store went into operation just before the financial crisis in 1998 after a seven-year legal battle. The renovation work had begun in 1996.

Owner/director Nina Grigoryevna relaxes in her immense, nearly empty office, which echoes like a church. She's an elegant blond woman of great youthfulness, wearing tailored slacks and high-heeled shoes—probably Italian design. Behind her leather armchair, which rolls on casters, are several brightly colored icons.

"My goal was to put this store back to business. Neither the minister of commerce of the city of Moscow nor the mayor of Moscow, Yuri Luzhkov, who were both present at the opening, thought I could do it. In convincing the banks to give me credit I knew that I was going to find myself in competition with other large establishments that had been in the business for a long time. I had to go all the way up to President Yeltsin, whom I had occasion to speak with personally. I made a point of saying that I wanted to preserve the outer appearance of Gastronome. The other potential buyers all intended to transform it radically, which worked against them.

"We are still paying back our loans. I pay my employees very well. I provide them with lunch and give them the right to a certain number of products each month. I always make it a point of honor to surround myself with a good team so that my personnel feel good about their work. I helped myself even more before the closing [for renovations, in 1992] by keeping the team together, continuing to pay some of their wages so that they wouldn't be tempted to take jobs elsewhere. Our country is full of good people. But you have to know how to use them. Life under Communism was certainly difficult, but some aspects of our lives, like job security, were much appreciated. Everything that has happened since then is so distressing."

When Nina Grigoryevna started to work as a saleswoman in the Gastronome in 1978, she was a little over thirty years old and an engineer by training. Divorce from her first husband prompted a change in lifestyle. Today, her two children are twenty-seven and twelve. The elder, a law student, has already given Nina two grandchildren.

"In the past, I was ashamed to acknowledge that I worked in trade. My engineering and physics studies gave me a superiority complex. My first job here was taking orders. In those days, we sold caviar and all kinds of other luxury products that the USSR was never short of until the beginning of the eighties."

Nina Grigoryevna acknowledges that these years of fights with city hall on one hand and with the building management on the other to acquire Gastronome were the toughest of her life. However, she also won't provide details.

"This building is very complex. What's more, it is difficult to get along with people who think only of themselves and their close relations. During all the renovations, I had to lock horns with the building authorities many times. Given their intransigence, I was forced to take action without their approval and at my own expense to replace the entire plumbing system of the supermarket. I invested everything in this building when there were only mice and dust here!

"My goal is to be considered one of Moscow's top supermarkets. I would like my assortments to be the best, and that my fish and wine departments have the best reputation. My window dressings don't attract the eye enough yet. I'm going to fix that. As for the corner pharmacy, it is still not a success. Before it I tried a cafeteria, but that didn't work, either. My Italian tables and chairs have been relegated to the cellar. But we're making progress. Today, I am free to make of this store whatever seems right to me. As long as I have strength and health, I will be here. I have grown up in this store. It is my reason for living."

In the end, the businesswoman reveals a few select confidences. Besides the retail trade, she is driven by something else: "I have always taken pleasure in helping others—helping somebody to stop drinking, helping a child study. I come from a family of very religious doctors who always prayed—even though I admit that when I was small, I prayed hardest to pass my examinations. Everything comes from the will of God. I am sure of it. If I leave this earth, that is the will of the Lord, too. The Gastronome is my cross! I will not be able to lower my prices until all my debts are paid off, most likely a year and a half from now. Only then will I be able to retire and engage full-time in politics!"

She laughs.

"The idea never occurred to me to leave this country, because I love Russia—the snow, the winter—and yet I've traveled the world. For me, perestroika meant the chance to make this country a more livable place. I don't know quite how to define myself. Yes, I 'do business,' but in a way, it is almost all about legalities. In any case, I would not dare to violate the law. Besides, I'm trying to help the Orthodox church as best I can. For example, I'm rebuilding a chapel about two hundred and fifty miles from Moscow.

"My children have completely different values from mine because they live in a different world. Even though they are not very experienced, they know that salvation is in the faith. I was somewhat distant from them when I was busy rebuilding this store. Then I wanted to be closer and I tried to repair the relationship. Family is the basis of everything. It must not be neglected."

PART TWO

THE APARTMENT MUSEUMS

CHAPTER 7

CENTRAL SECTION, FOURTEENTH FLOOR:
THE TRUBNIKOV AND BULICHIOV FAMILIES

Two elevators open on the fourteenth floor to a wide oval landing with pale green walls. The parquet floors are worn and scuffed. The light, once provided by elegant ceiling fixtures, is white neon. Four imposing wood doors face the elevator in a semicircle, all identical. A fifth door, without a handle (stolen, like so many others), opens onto a dingy staircase.

These four apartments have been occupied by families who moved in shortly after the vysotka was opened in 1952 and represented those privileged members of Soviet society who were invited to move into the skyscraper on Ironmongers Quay. They included a military engineer, a military attorney, a well-known astronomer (though never a Party member), and an academic specializing in construction. Today their descendants—the second and third generations—still live in their apartments.

Elena Parfionova is the daughter of the military attorney. She was once a professor of Arabic at the Central Committee School of the Communist Party and still interprets Arabic on the radio. Her mother was also an Arabic translator and attended all sorts of international conferences.

Viktor Abramsev, fifty-three, is the son of the aforementioned military engineer, who hanged himself from a chandelier in his apartment a few months after moving in. Viktor's mother, Nina Sergeyevna, herself an engineer, became a dressmaker. She did this secretly, because it was forbidden to operate a private business at home. Viktor became a mechanic, and today he lives in a dacha and rents out his apartment in the vysotka.

Katya Trubnikova, sixty-six, is the granddaughter of the astronomer mentioned earlier. Katya lived a large part of her life in the apartment next to Viktor Abramsev, which had originally been allocated to her grandfather in 1952. Then she arranged an exchange with her neighbors, the Bulichiovs. She now lives with her aunt and her son Sergey, forty, an artist, in two rooms that she had once rented out.

Andrei Bulichiov, fifty-six, is an engineer, and the son of the aforementioned academic, who moved into their apartment in 1952. In 1979, however, Andrei and his wife, Irina, exchanged apartments with Katya. The Bulichiovs live with their son in the Moscow suburbs and rent their apartment to a foreigner.

Katya Trubnikova is still a very beautiful woman with a smooth, delicate but lively face. She remains discreet about her personal life. Shortly after her marriage in 1958, her husband, a doctor in the military, was assigned to a post in the easternmost part of Russia. He stayed there for twenty-five years. Katya refused to follow him, and the couple divorced five years after their marriage. She never rebuilt her life. Mostly Katya likes to talk about her maternal grandfather, who educated her (her father was killed in the war) and whom she still adores:

"My grandfather was a member of the International Union of Astronomers. In 1943 he was director of the Institute of Astronomy but lived in a four-room basement apartment with his two daughters and his granddaughters. Doctors advised him to move for his health. He was seventy-two years old when he moved into this skyscraper, where he lived only five more years.

"We moved into our apartment on October 8, 1952. The weather was very nice, I remember. The biggest problem was transporting our library. It consisted of an enormous amount of books and we had to use many cars. At first, we were afraid to look out of the windows because we were not used to being so high up. We had decided to install Grandpa in the middle room, which was painted pink. 'There is no way I will stay in this boudoir,' he raged, and finally chose the first room, painted pistachio green, which became his bedroom and office. He slept on an iron cot.

"In those days, the immense garage was almost empty. My grandfather bought a Pobeda [a post–World War II car whose name meant "victory"], and a chauffeur took him to and from the institute. Everyone was amazed that the director of an institute had his own business car. When he died, we had to sell the Pobeda because keeping it in the garage here became too costly."

Katya has saved all the documents from 1952, including an occupancy order dated October 3 and cosigned by her grandfather, a Directive No. 15, and a detailed inventory of the apartment.

"I've been trying to put my grandfather's papers in order. In the letters he wrote to his future wife at the turn of the century, he touched on all sorts of subjects: Socialism, Buddhism and other religions, the political situation. I wish my son Sergey could turn it into a book. I've also saved all his personal files—

sold a few after his death—and the Lenin Library [now called the National Library of the Russian Federation] has preserved all his correspondence, which I would like to recover."

She points at photographs of him when he was just beginning his career as a teaching assistant at the Moscow Observatory.

"He was the first astronomer to receive the Stalin Prize. My mother and my aunt were afraid of him because he would never repeat what he had just said. He showed more leniency with his granddaughters."

The Bulichiov family, by contrast, seems more irreverent, even though Andrei's father also received the illustrious Stalin Prize.

"When you receive it, you need to say thanks to the Lord," Andrei says ironically, an unlit cigarette in his hand, sitting at a Formica-covered kitchen table of the apartment that he rents in the suburbs. He does not seem to be at ease.

"As a scholar, my father was singled out for his scientific works in the field of construction." He illustrates the statement with many medals neatly arranged in cases lined in red velvet like those in which silverware is stored.

"We initially obtained two rooms in a large apartment community in the center of Moscow, but my mother, true Polish lady that she was, couldn't stand the lack of privacy and went to live in a dacha in the outskirts. We moved into this vysotka in September 1953. There was one broken tile in the kitchen wall from which I used to watch the few cars leaving or entering the garage. I was fascinated and scared to death at the same time. Everyone on the fourteenth floor was. The garages were built by prisoners. They were finished shortly after we moved in. The men sometimes threw love letters in bottles weighted with stones to the young shop girls from the ground floor who dared to approach them. After one of these bottles hit a child in the head, the young women weren't allowed to go near the garages anymore.

"I never felt that I lived in a place for privileged people, or that my buddies were special. I do, however, remember Ira's [his wife's] expression when I told her where I lived. She immediately wanted to marry me!" He laughs. "It was indeed an unthinkable type of home for the average Soviet citizen. People stepped inside and their eyes opened wide—the immense hall, the elevators made of precious wood, the marble, the frescos!

"I finally left the vysotka in the early nineties because our financial situation was complicated. I don't know if we will ever move back. I am six years away from retirement. My monthly pension will be around sixty dollars. How are we going to make it? For the time being, I have no choice. We must rent the apartment out.

"Thirty years ago, when I started to work in the Institute of Construction, which was transformed into a joint stock company in 1992, it employed nine hundred and fifty people. Today there are no more than ninety-six. As a project manager, I directed a team of forty-five people, which got reduced little by little. In 1994, I was placed on unpaid leave for five years. Under the Soviet regime, we constructed gigantic chemical complexes. Today, we build villages of cottages for new Russians. Why? Because there is nothing else to do. You have to adapt to the demand."

During the nineties, Katya Trubnikova and her family also had to reconcile themselves to leaving their apartment. In 1994, after having worked for almost forty years as a biologist (hematologist) specializing in the treatment of cancer, she was, she says, forced to take her retirement.

"Although as a highly specialized researcher my wages were twice the national average, my pension is insignificant," she observes. "And on top of that, inflation and the various monetary reforms have frittered away our last savings."

In 1992, she and her neighbor Viktor made a passageway between their two-room apartments and rented the combined space to foreigners for a high price. The rent, paid in dollars, allowed Katya, her son, and her elderly aunt to survive and also helped Viktor's family. In 1995, Katya took back her apartment, which once again became a "two-room."

Today all the residents of the fourteenth floor feel nostalgic about the vysotka's "lost status." They deplore the general carelessness that prevails today, viewing it as a corollary of the "democratization" of the country. "Fortunately, President Putin is in the process of fixing it," says one, referring to the country, not the vysotka.

They regret the need for a doorkeeper downstairs, seated in front of a pathetic little round table ("today it would be found in an ordinary dacha") on which a telephone is enthroned, who won't let anyone pass without inquiring about their destination. In 1991, doorkeepers disappeared for a while and, to the huge dismay of the "elite" of the vysotka's inhabitants, tramps moved onto the immense staircases. Then there were no more elevator operators, who had functioned as a second line of defense.

Today, according to Katya, one cannot even call them elevators anymore. Instead they are "freight hoists that constantly break down."

Also gone are the red carpets that used to be rolled out in the entrance hall for all Party functions, however minor. Even the rings in the floor to which the carpets were attached no longer exist. And what about that employee from the Valia Bakery who made "round bread" every morning? She used to promenade on the floors with her immense loaves. Where has she gone?

"You could order whatever you wanted," Katya remembers with a smile.

What they miss most of all is the conviviality. On Saturday afternoons, after fending off the caretakers and neighbors, the younger generation sometimes organized dance parties. And the end-of-year festivities were unforgettable, too. Everyone began the evening at home with their own guests. Then, a little before midnight, the four apartment doors were opened and everyone mingled on the landing and went into one another's homes.

"I'd go looking for my father or my mother in the neighbors' apartments," Katya recalls. "Somewhere, my aunt was playing the piano. We sang and danced together until morning."

Neither parents nor children spoke a word about work or politics.

CHAPTER 8

CENTRAL SECTION, TWELFTH FLOOR:
ANATOLY AND IRINA BORISOVICH

It's a frigid February evening, and I'm happy to be jammed into a small paneled room in the "house-museum" of poet Sergey Yessinin, nestled among the renovated office buildings of the banking district in the center of Moscow. Yessinin (1895–1925) wrote mostly about the Russian countryside and remains considerably popular. He committed suicide. About thirty people are in attendance at a free recital dedicated to the poet.

Looking dashing in his tuxedo, Anatoly Borisovich readjusts his bow tie before making his entrance. In the days of the Soviet Union, there would be hundreds, sometimes even thousands of spectators who came to listen to the verses of great poets being recited. Tonight the audience fits into a small room in this historic house. There's not even a stage. Only a narrow aisle separates Anatoly from the small gathering.

In the front row, a chubby, braided eight-year-old girl keeps rummaging through her shiny little plastic bag, a replica of her mother's, trying to extract a miniature mirror. At this precise moment, Anatoly Borisovich strides "onstage," a big smile on his lips, completely at ease. He launches into the poetry, his right hand in his pocket, the left accentuating the verses with grand gestures.

When Anatoly Borisovich finishes, a young man takes over, starting to sing, accompanied on the piano by his wife in a long silvery sheath gown. Right in the middle of a musical phrase, the young man unexpectedly rushes out of the room. The pianist continues to play. Vaguely disconcerted, the audience members shift in their seats. The young man returns at the end of the piece. "Please excuse my sentimentality, but the words of the fourth verse move me so much each time I sing them that it makes me cry," he explains.

The couple moves on to more upbeat tunes and the audience relaxes. Meanwhile, the little girl has found a minitube of lipstick and happily daubs at her mouth, so preoccupied that she doesn't notice that the contents of her purse are falling off her lap and noisily all over the floor.

The recitations by Anatoly Borisovich alternate with the musical renditions by the young couple. After reading another poem, Borisovich addresses the room in a clear and poised voice: "I have loved the poetry of Yessinin since I was thirteen years old. He died so young, but his poetry is still alive. Every one of his verses is courageous and so extraordinarily visionary. It is as if he had written about us, about our fatherland of today."

He begins reciting again. Suddenly he wrinkles his eyebrows and yanks his right hand from his pocket. His lips freeze in an expression of confusion. Silence. The words do not come—he has forgotten a verse! He is finally rescued by a man in the back row, sitting among Yessinin enthusiasts who know every one of their idol's lines. When the poem is finished, they all warmly applaud the recitation of "master of the word" Anatoly Borisovich Sviensky, "Actor Emeritus of Russia." (Actor Emeritus is a somewhat less glorious title than People's Artist, which among other perks entitles its recipient to a luxury car that will take him or her to and from performances.)

At the reception following the performance, the museum's director keeps on proposing toasts even after glasses have been emptied. Then Anatoly Borisovich returns to his apartment in the vysotka on Ironmongers Quay, a crumpled fifty-ruble bill (less than two dollars) in his pocket. He is anguished at the idea of giving it to his wife.

"It's so little, she will surely make some remark. Still," he adds, "it's better than nothing. She always accuses me of working for free!" He sighs.

My conversation with this professional actor who specializes in poetry recitals and his wife, Ira, takes place in their dining room, which is encumbered with pieces of old furniture, including an immense grand piano on which sits a vase with several dozen dried and crumbling flowers.

"I am the great-great-grandson by marriage of the Polish poet Adam Mickiewicz. Like all supposed 'Russians,' I am the product of four different bloodlines. I am twenty-five percent Russian, twenty-five percent Polish, twelve-point-five percent Lithuanian, and thirty-seven-point-five percent Ukrainian. On my grandfather Borislav's side, my ancestors are Polish-Lithuanians, lawyers from father to son going back to 1576, graduates of the University of Vilnius. They lived in the city of Brest-Litovsk for a long time, where the border with Poland is today. Borislav was married to the daughter of the eldest son of Mickiewicz. My family tree fills three books, going as far back as Catherine the Second. This helps me to account for things my father tried to keep hidden from me.

"We've lived in this vysotka since 1969. Before that I lived with my father near a church with a very interesting history. It had been closed in 1932 but was reopened in 1992. I fought for nine years to get it reopened. Today I still contribute to its restoration. The administrative offices of the patriarchate of Moscow were located a few hundred yards away, but no one from there ever did anything to help us. As far as I know, this is the third religious structure built on this same site. The first went up during the reign of Ivan the Terrible, the second in the seventeenth century. This third one was built by a Frenchman, Nicholas Legrand, who came to Russia during the French Revolution. This is the only church in Moscow with two bell towers.

"I want to tell you why we moved here in 1969. It's lucky that Ira can't hear us, because she doesn't like it when I talk. [In fact, Ira seems to be occupied in answering the telephone.] I needed the prestige of living here. As a theater director and poetry reciter, it was necessary for me to host parties, and this apartment suited that purpose perfectly. There was nothing like it to impress an opera director or orchestra leader and other people of that stature. This impressive hall and the stairs leading to the elevators had the same effect on them as when a peasant enters a cathedral. The building still impresses people. I had to struggle for more than a year and a half, after eight successive exchanges, before I finally got this apartment. No question about it. I only agreed to live in the main section/hall of the building to get the full benefit of the luxurious entrance. Ira does not want me to boast about it. She finds it ridiculous.

"I never was a Communist or a Pioneer [member of the Communist youth organization]. To the contrary, between 1929 and 1932 I studied at what is called 'alternative school' along with future dissident Andrey Sakharov. [Andrey Sakharov recounts in his memoirs that for three years a private tutor came to his house to give him lessons and that his parents gathered on their premises, on these occasions, two or three other children so they could also benefit from this instruction.] Our parents were colleagues in the physical sciences at Moscow State University. To avoid being enrolled in the regular program, we had to pretend we had a disability. Even today, I wonder why my parents were not arrested. They took so many risks, among them keeping me from attending Soviet schools. In this alternative program, our instructors, who were all graduates of elitist, formerly czarist schools, were extraordinary. They taught me Greek and Roman mythology, philosophy, religion, mathematics, and German. There were a dozen of us, but we met sporadically, so as not to attract the attention of the authorities or of our neighbors. The courses took place in one apartment or another.

"Ever since I was very small, my parents taught me how to lead a double life, official and unofficial. Now I do it effortlessly. The authorities demanded that I recite verses for the celebration of the one hundredth anniversary of Stalin's birth in 1979. How could I refuse? Am I anxious to end my days in Magadan [a town in Siberia famous for its gulags]? I complied, but that doesn't mean I believe. No, I never did believe!" He suppresses a laugh.

"I compare the current period with that of the NEP [New Economic Policy, instituted by Lenin in 1921 and shut down by Stalin in 1929], when everything was for sale, when kiosks overflowed the sidewalks, and when many poor made a decent living, just like today. One of them, who lived not far from my father's place, had a very beautiful voice."

Anatoly Borisovich begins to sing a song about a beggar, until a coughing fit stops him.

"Ira refuses to let me give recitals without being paid. The main thing is that I like doing it, especially because it pleases the audience. I know perfectly well that our line of work has no future, but being a reciter is like playing in a comedy. You have to be both a poet and an actor at the same time. It's total freedom, the hardest part being to hold the public's attention."

To illustrate this, Anatoly Borisovich begins to recite a poem by Lermontov. Ira, who has finished her telephone conversation, returns and bursts out laughing when she hears it. When he stumbles through the last verse, she cuts in savagely: "Officially, we are retired, but we continue to slave away. We are often invited to perform at benefit functions. Me, I never accept, but my husband—always. A cleaning lady gets paid better! To use public toilets costs five rubles, so I don't see why a highly skilled artist should have to appear for free. Two years ago, for the two hundredth anniversary of Pushkin's birth, we were invited to appear at the Duma. Tolya recited Pushkin, of course. So did I, as well as poems by Anna Akhmatova. But the organizers behaved like boors. Nobody sent a car for us and we had no place to dress or put on makeup. What's more, neither of us was paid, or offered a cup of coffee, or driven back to our house after a presentation that lasted more than three hours!"

"My wife and I have different points of view about this," says Anatoly Borisovich. "Onstage, I never think about money."

The phone rings and Ira goes to answer it. She hangs up on the caller and comes right back.

"How many free recitals did we give in Soviet times? Back

then, we could do it because we earned a lot of money, and our profession was popular up until the eighties. Forty years ago, poets like Yevgeny Yevtushenko, Andrey Voznesensky, and Bulat Okudjava wrote marvelous verses, and the public clamored to hear them. Later, we were authorized to recite the verses of Marina Tsvetaeva, of Anna Akhmatova, or of Nikolay Gumiliov—that was a real success! We worked out the smallest details of our recital with the best theater directors. I had trained to be an actress, but I quit acting and concentrated on recitation because it was more interesting than theater. In the theater, we were always extremely dependent on the repertoire, on the theater director, and on the cast. When I decided to recite Akhmatova, on the other hand, I could choose my own director—that's total freedom!

"But it was very difficult to get permission to recite Akhmatova or Bulgakov. The minister of culture couldn't see why we made a point of reciting 'The White Guard' [describing those who fought against the Bolsheviks. Because of it, Bulgakov was accused of being "anti-Soviet"]. The bureaucrats were afraid of losing their jobs and thought that what we call 'culture' was not worthy of Soviet might. The USSR used to have one hundred official 'reciters.' The state could decide to send whoever it wanted to recite in a school or a performance hall.

"But we were never one of those. Nor was I ever a Communist, and not being a registered Party member was enormously harmful to our respective careers. Tolya was accused of continuing to believe in God and practice his religion, and never received the high distinction of 'People's Artist.'

"Today we live humbly, but all intellectuals live humbly. We can't afford to pay for show tickets. As for television, we don't watch it, because they only show garbage. For lovers of true art, all that is shocking.

"The other day I went to the Polytechnic Museum to ask how much it would cost to stage a recital in their auditorium. At first, the people there didn't recognize me; then they apologized when I introduced myself. They told me that they rent the hall for four hundred dollars an evening. When I told them that was too much, they seemed disappointed. Today, we do our productions wherever we can find a roof!"

Surrounded by photographs, she turns to the past:

"Tolya and I have known each other since we were fifteen. We met in 1948, on a train. He saw me, approached, and started to tell me about his life. He claimed he was famous, that he was an actor who only took leading roles. I kept quiet. He immediately irritated me. I eventually told him that I was also an actress. He courted me for two years."

She gets up again to answer the phone, which seems to never stop ringing, and Anatoly Borisovich picks up the thread: "At the time, I worked and lived in Klaipeda [Vilnius, the capital of Lithuania]. I was also in love with a young Lithuanian actress."

Irina's reappearance cuts off that subject. Tolya returns to the story of their first meeting: "There used to be enormous train convoys between Lithuania and Kazakhstan. During a stop in Smolensk, while we were sauntering along the platform, I asked Ira for her telephone number. Later I called her in Moscow and reminded her of our walk in Smolensk. I was just preparing to go back there again for a show and wanted her to accompany me. Later, we appeared onstage together."

When Ira leaves the room again, he whispers conspiratori-
ally, "The poet Gumiliov was right when he said of himself and
Akhmatova, 'It's a miracle that we have not separated.' Nothing
is more difficult than two artists living together, especially
when one of them is such a character!"

Ira returns, but the phone rings once again and she runs
off to answer it. When she returns again, she tells her husband
that they need to go to the Mosfilm [state film production
bureaucracy] studios the next day. This immediately raises the
inevitable problem of transportation, because they don't have a
car, the subway stations are far away, and taxis are expensive.

"We didn't have children because we devoted all of our
lives to the theater," Irina says, "so it's very hard as we get old.
For now, we are together, but what will happen when one of us
is gone?" Her usually sonorous and controlled voice sounds
anguished.

Tolya doesn't breathe a word. His head is lowered.

"We are all equal in the face of death," he finally says.

"We are always alone in our coffin," Irina nearly shouts,
then calms down a bit. "Still, we must admit that though our
life was very hard, our parents' was harder."

She becomes even more animated.

"I always dreamed of becoming an actress. I had just finished school in the summer of 1941, and the end-of-year prom
had taken place. I was attracted to lots of boys but thought of
only one thing—becoming an actress. I wanted to have a place
of my own, my own career, an interesting life.

"One clear evening in August, I found myself in Red
Square with a young man. We were walking quietly when all of

a sudden he mentioned the possibility that the Soviet Union would enter the war. I absolutely did not believe it, because we had just signed a pact with Hitler. I wanted him to speak to me about love instead.

"The next day, my father woke me up, shouting, 'Aren't you ashamed to sleep through a war?' We had entered into war during the night! *My God, what will become of Moscow, my beloved city? I never had another,* I immediately thought. I was afraid of foreigners, of the unknown, of war. They had already built barricades in the streets. My father, an architect and structural engineer, soon left for Lithuania with my sister and my mother, but I refused to leave. I wanted to stay in Moscow and become an actress. I registered myself in a factory that was soon being evacuated also. I didn't know what else I could do to avoid leaving. I thought of going to the front to defend my fatherland. I was convinced that life in the Soviet Union was the best anywhere. However, hundreds were dying at the front each day.

"I did not go to the front. Until 1942 I worked in Ulyanovsk as a nurse. I was in charge of laying out the dead. We worked in a stinking cellar. Everyone smoked. That's where I started smoking. [She still does.] I was obsessed with the idea of becoming 'somebody.' My one and only goal was to return to Moscow and resume my studies. One night, I climbed into the last car in a train that was transporting tanks and hid inside one of them. They discovered me during a stop. Passing from one train to another, I finally arrived in Moscow.

"My parents' former apartment in the Arbat [historic neighborhood in the center of the city] had been taken over by strangers, so I had to sleep on a trunk in a corner of the corridor.

I went to beg to be registered for the entrance exams at the Theatrical Institute, where I presented myself without any preparation. I recited an extract from *War and Peace* and from Lermontov. I got so swept up in it, I couldn't stop! The members of the jury had to interrupt me to tell me that I had been accepted! That's how my career began. You have to want to be somebody—you have to really want it.

"Recently, I sold all of our old things, including some fabrics, to buy a studio in the suburbs. We have practically nothing left, but we intend to rent this apartment, furnished, for three hundred dollars per month. We don't know if we'll still be alive in a year, or in two years, or in ten, but I don't see why we can't spend them tranquilly, without major problems."

She leaves the room again, as if exhausted by the effort this performance has taken.

"Ira is right, even though she nags me all the time," Tolya says eventually. "She often gets upset. It's a female characteristic. Of course I understand that, but it's still very difficult to live with. Having said that, I, too, always dreamed of doing what I did. When I was young, I could perform *George Dandin* by Molière in French!"

Irina returns. "Life is hard, but it's still beautiful," she announces.

CHAPTER 9

An old man in a jogging outfit reclines on a living room sofa. His face is wrinkled, but his eyes are youthful. On the little finger of his left hand is a silver signet ring with a snake, which represents a trickster, and a lion, which symbolizes strength, fighting over a magnificent diamond set in the middle.

"This ring has been passed from father to son in my family for two hundred years," he explains. The walls of his apartment are covered with souvenirs. A grand piano partially blocks the passageway.

In another room, his fourth wife, Alla, who is forty-four years younger than he, is watching television. She has finished cooking the meal she made "to celebrate our nine years of living together." She wants me to watch a video of a group of popular young musicians who have taken songs written by her husband and turned them into hits. The old man hastens to join us, shuffling his small slippered feet and squinting at the bluish screen.

"Ah, yes, that's amusing. They seem to like my music," he mumbles, then returns to the living room to smoke another Camel. He offers one to me.

Everyone I interviewed in the vysotka spoke about Bogoslovsky in terms either respectful or disgusted. The poet Vozne-sensky's wife, Zoya, remembers Bogoslovsky as a practical joker. Knowing she had guests coming one night, he apparently once called to warn her that the water would be cut off for two days. She rushed around filling all the containers in the house with water. It turned out to be one of his usual jokes.

I also sensed a sort of indulgence toward him, despite the fact that some suspected him of collaborating with the KGB, beginning in World War II (which would explain why he enjoyed such great freedom of movement, especially abroad). But when I ask him whether he informed on people or contributed to their being sent to the labor camps in the gulag, I can't get a straight answer. He tells a joke or a story to distract me from the subject.

"In Paris, I always stayed at the Hotel Seine, where every-one knew me. Every year, along with the Soviet minister of culture, I met my French colleagues. Sometimes, very rarely however, the composers Francis Lemarque and Philippe Ge-rard came to the Soviet Union. In 1957, during the World Youth Festival, Francis Lemarque wanted to meet the com-poser of the famous song 'Dark Night.' Me, in other words. I don't know where this love for France comes from. Probably from my family, who were members of the Saint Petersburg aristocracy and spoke fluent French.

"I moved into this vysotka when it opened in 1952. First I lived in Wing VK; then, two years later, after the birth of my son, I was offered this apartment in Wing V. I had complained about not having enough room. In two days, they found me this three-room apartment! Every piece of furniture was con-structed according to the designs drafted by my first wife. That's why this apartment is unique."

Alla brings us coffee on a tray. She asks her husband not to forget his special sugar.

"Did you bring the vodka?" he quips with a smile. "Nothing has changed here for several decades, and that has protected me from agitation. I have never had any occupation other than composing music or of literature. I am the author of nine books of humor, as well as two satirical novels. Today, I prefer literature. I did, however, write fifteen of the most well known melodies in all of Russia. I started composing before the war. The composers of today, I really don't understand them, and most of all I hate their amateurism. Three chords on the guitar repeated over and over cannot claim to revolutionize music! Their songs are ninety-nine percent remakes of old songs. That's why they never really become hits. My tunes are still in the hearts of my fellow citizens.

"I was glad to come live in this vysotka because it was a great privilege to be given one of these apartments. Besides, I already had acquaintances here: the writer Alexander Tvardovsky, the famous documentary filmmaker Roman Karmen—after his death, his wife married Vassily Aksionov—the ballerina Galina Ulanova, the actresses Ladynina and Smirnova, the lion tamer Irina Bugrimova, and the poets Andrei Voznesensky and Yevgeny Yevtushenko, whose wife Galia I always detested. She still lives here.

"I have my own circle of friends—for the most part artists, writers, and musicians. I don't know anybody else in this building and I don't speak to anybody anymore. I still work and don't want to be disturbed.

"My wife Alla is a graduate of the conservatory, like me. Though we are not from the same generation, she is also a composer, so we speak the same language—that of music. My forty-nine-year-old son also lives in Moscow. He graduated from the Institute of Literature and from the conservatory. He has written two novels and composed an opera."

The walls of the living room give evidence of past glory. There is a painting given to Bogoslovsky by Panitch, a well-known Yugoslav artist. There are lots of sketches and caricatures. There are photographs of a young man sitting at the piano, surrounded by Soviet celebrities. A framed diploma from the International Order of Arts bears the inscription: "Awarded for Services Rendered to the Arts and Franco-Soviet Friendship." There is a huge drawing in black and white by the French artist Jean Marais, signed by Marais and with an inscription in French. Bogoslovsky carefully repositions a perfume bottle shaped according to a sketch by Jean Marais, obviously very proud of it. He leans forward to draw my attention to another special vase. When he bends down to search for something in a lower cupboard I'm afraid that he won't be able to get up again, but he does, victoriously waving an operatic score that he wrote with his son, Andrei. The television continues to blare in the background, but he ignores it.

"I chaired the Franco-Soviet Friendship Association for quite a long time. However, politics never interested me. An ironic glance works much better. I sometimes believed life was a dream, because so much of mine seemed incredible to me. In 1977, the Institute of Astronomy proclaimed me godfather of a star that now carries my name. What an honor! I told Yuri Luzhkov that I would move to my star if he continued to raise the fees on my apartment. Luzhkov responded with that line of poetry that goes, 'If that ever happens, take me with you.'

Humor has always been my salvation. It has protected me from many excesses and hangovers."

Bogoslovsky wants to sneak a smoke without Alla knowing it. He pulls out a pack of cigarettes he had stashed under a cushion.

"At school in Saint Petersburg we learned to compose without the piano. We only used it for especially complicated chords. So my theatrical Fifth Symphony was entirely written without accompaniment. For a long time, the Saint Petersburg Philharmonic Orchestra refused to play it, on the pretext that it had been written by a 'hooligan'! At the time, they were performing nothing but Shostakovich. So the orchestra was only moderately successful, the public being unprepared for this style of music. They really only put it onto playlists ten years later.

"My songs helped the USSR because they were good, that's all! But I really don't like that 'Dark Night' anymore. It's been played for fifty years—I'm tired of it. When I was young, I wanted to invent a new kind of music in which each instrument, with its own intonations, would reproduce the sound of a conversation, intermingling musical discussions on different topics—like telephone conversations between friends. Right now I'm working on an opera in one act using this very style. A tuba goes to a government office for an apartment. He is accompanied by an oboe, which, with an Oriental intonation, tries to slip a bribe to the bureaucrat represented by a trombone. A clarinet, the trombone's secretary, interrupts, joins them, and so forth. Using instruments to represent humans interests me more and more."

Alla interrupts, brandishing a photo in which her husband

and the French musician Michel Legrand, both very young, are seated at a piano. There's another picture of the same men two years ago, at a music festival in Kiev. Then, last but not least, there is a photo of Bogoslovsky with Pres. Boris Yeltsin, from when the composer was given an award in 1995.

The bells of a nearby monastery start to ring, loudly. The composer doesn't seem to hear them. He turns to politics:

"Our country is not really stable yet, but do you have stability in France? Will Jacques Chirac remain president? And what is going on with that crazy Le Pen? Does he still have a chance? Whatever became of the Communists? And is it good that the franc no longer exists? Doesn't this cause suffering for anybody? How did the transition occur? Have valuations and prices stayed the same? Is it like a European dollar, this euro? In Russia, the dollar remains king.

"I read someplace about some people who got arrested for making counterfeit currency." That makes him laugh. "I don't even know the name of the first secretary of your Communist Party—is it George Marchais? The Communists are no longer a political force in France. That doesn't surprise me. It was bound to happen. Those dimwits. Didn't they realize that our Communists, in spite of their pitiful attempts to remain as a political force, caused disaster? I knew Gorbachev well when he was a low-level civil servant and Party functionary. Even though his first attempts at change were not bad, as a policy it turned out to be inadequate. Too bad!"

As a matter of principle, I refuse to pay for interviews, which the residents of the building all agreed, without complaint, to give me for free. I made an exception for Bogoslovsky because his testimony seemed important to get and I wanted to see if his wife would insist upon my honoring her request. By telephone, before my interview with her husband, she had requested $200 per hour. I negotiated that down to $70 for more than two hours. Two other people who would have deserved to be included in this work requested to be paid, but I did not interview them. Alla gives me an inquiring look, so I hand over the money she is charging me for this interview with her husband. She counts the green bills silently. Then she gets up quickly and puts them on the piano and sits down to play a piece she recently composed for her husband—a romantic melody. There will be a small "jubilee" celebration in his honor at the House of Artists. She keeps rhythm with her head, and a refrain rises, partly in French: "Oh, Nikita, don't leave me, Nikita/Oh, Nikita, don't leave me . . ."

Alla sings well and with genuine emotion. Behind her, sitting stiffly, the old composer listens. When she stops, he applauds gently.

"So you didn't forget it?" she asks him mysteriously and a bit ironically. It is very hard to pierce the mask that this couple hides behind.

When we say good-bye, Alla adds, "Do come and stay with us if you have need of a roof some night." She has forgotten that I live in the vysotka, too.

CHAPTER 10

Of all the inhabitants of the vysotka on Ironmongers Quay, his slender outline is perhaps the most recognizable. Whatever the weather, this bearded beanpole of a man walks his four borzois three times a day, braving the icy cold with them. The dogs are as thin and delicate-looking as their master. Constantly shivering, pressed close together, the elegant animals glide through the halls of the building like shadows, with an absorbed and haughty air, before disappearing through the heavy swinging carved wooden doors of the entryway. On their heels is their master, Vladimir Kossytkin, a professor of drawing and design.

He uses his apartment as a workshop, and every inch is covered with paintings, drawings, and sketches. A long trestle table is positioned in front of the window, through which one can distinguish tiny figures crossing the bridge over the river separating the vysotka from the Kremlin far below. Cars look like toys from this height. Models of skulls are interspersed among a variety of sculptures, the works of his students. What looks at first like a bunched fur blanket monopolizing the threadbare sofa is actually one of the greyhounds. Even the cat doesn't seem to know where to put itself.

"I've lived in this building since 1952. My father was a former border guard who became the deputy chief of the Kremlin guard, a post he occupied from 1935 until his death two weeks before Stalin's [1953]. Before moving here, we lived inside the Kremlin, in a staff apartment that has long since been destroyed. Kids had a lot of fun there, especially when they gave us permission to ride a toboggan in the Alexandrovsky Garden for an hour. Still, we lived a military life, like in a fort.

"I was eleven years old when we moved into this immense and empty building that resembled a monument. We couldn't make noise. It was even worse than within the Kremlin, where at least I had some soldier friends. And to make things worse, the kids in the district called us the *vysotniki* [those who live in the vysotka], which infuriated me. They treated us with mistrust and skepticism.

"My father was hostage to the system but knew that Stalin's regime would end badly. Unfortunately, he only lived in this building, which he adored, for three months. He often took me to watch the huge parades in Red Square. I even saw Comrade Stalin there, close up. I was very disappointed. He was already a withered old man with a pockmarked face. His white tunic swam on his body. In the pictures he seemed to have such strength."

"My father also took me to Lenin's mausoleum, sometimes even at night. One evening we walked in and I saw an enormous man with a bloated scarlet face and red hands. My father poured some liquid from a container. To my horror, I realized that they were going to drink a toast! They emptied their glasses in one gulp. Afterward we entered into a very dark room where there was a guard and I saw Lenin laid out.

"My father was nice when he was in a good mood, but if

not he could be terrible. Still, I adored him. He never stopped
inventing activities for me, and outings.

"His death in 1953 was a great loss, and a catastrophe for
our family. He was forty-nine years old. My mother was left
with three children to raise alone. She was courageous and did
everything she could to educate us as best as she could. Luckily we were able to keep the three-room situated on the fifth
floor of the right sector because it was registered.

"My father loved the Kremlin, and he was so delighted to be
able to admire it from his own window. His family was from
Saratov, on the Volga River, but he was orphaned very young.
After he met my mother at a meeting of the Young Communists
organization, they lived together without ever marrying, which
caused lots of problems after his death. My mother had to fight
for her rights. My father would undoubtedly have wished for me
to become a soldier, because, for him, that meant 'to be someone,' but he knew that it didn't interest me, and never would he
have forced me.

"I can't really say that he was happy. In retrospect, he was
always very concerned for us and our welfare. He entertained
friends at the house, artists and actors. His favorite author was
the humorist [Mikhail] Zochenko. We had a huge library. It
was as if he wanted to turn our living room into an intellectual
salon, which, however, it was not. My mother barely knew how
to read and expressed herself in her own astonishing language,
a mixture of Russian and Ukrainian. Her accent made everyone laugh.

"My military service lasted three years, from 1960 to 1963.
To my surprise, I felt rather comfortable in this context of
chronic vexations and various mortifications, undoubtedly be-

cause I had known it growing up. I liked it that everyone was treated the same way, that it had neither class nor caste.

"After the army, I tried my luck at the Institute of Design because I was interested in drawing and sculpture, but I wasn't admitted. Then, some Uzbeks, friends of my parents, invited me to Tashkent, where I went to attend the fine arts school.

"When I left for Tashkent, I thought it would be forever. The inhabitants there were so welcoming, and they were of all nationalities. There was even a Chinese Art Academy of Peking there! I lived in a student dormitory tucked away on a street that made me think of Montmartre in Paris. Nothing was expensive, the atmosphere was very Bohemian, and we artists all lived near one another. We put on a play by Bertolt Brecht, for which I constructed the sets. I spent two happy years there before I was asked to leave the school. My artistic experiments were not to the taste of my professors.

"I finally left Uzbekistan after the earthquake in the spring of 1966. The provincialism had begun to get to me. I thought I should be in the 'middle of the action,' where things were happening. I didn't really have a goal. I simply wanted to continue my experimentation.

"When I returned to Moscow, my many nephews and nieces had taken over the apartment in the vysotka. I had to rent a room downtown because I needed a place for my canvases. I knew that many artists lived here, but to me they were true lords, stars, out of reach!

"I was finally accepted at the Institute of Design in Moscow. I had trouble there with certain narrow-minded professors, though there were others who were geniuses. My mother had decided to take a job in the building to supplement her meager pension. I was upset about this decision, but she had no other choice. Like my father, she loved this vysotka and its residents. It was where she lived, and she felt safe here. She remained a committed Communist until her death. She was one of those people who idealized the Revolution and could never see things any other way. It was at the beginning of the Brezhnev years. Our building didn't interest anyone anymore and started to fall apart. That's when it became dearer to me—as if the monster had, so to speak, been tamed."

From the kitchen a female voice calls the dogs to come and eat, but the four borzois, flopped on the furniture of the front room and the studio and also on the parquet floor, do not budge until their master gets up. Then they stretch their seemingly endless legs and launch themselves like four bolts of lightning into the corridor.

"I started to teach painting and drawing at the Institute of Design after I stopped painting eight years ago. I still teach there. I consider myself a theorist of composition. The art school to which I belong is inspired by the so-called 'Vkhoutemas' movement, a unique postrevolutionary artistic school that was liquidated by the Bolshevik powers at the end of the twenties. Over the last ten years, our institute has become a shadow of its former self. Curiously, the majority of the teachers have not left their positions, even though they are hardly ever paid. It's because nobody works there for the money. Our teaching 'mission' is a true social vocation, though we all have second jobs in order to survive.

"Except for the Paris-Moscow exposition, and the very

politicized Moscow-Berlin show in 1993, Russian painting has scarcely produced anything during the last decade. As for me, I've worked like crazy to avoid getting stuck in the same doldrums in which our country finds itself. This seems to be the only way to survive. Finding a gallery to exhibit your work is not only very difficult; you have to pay. Today, you pay for everything.

"In 1996, when my mother died, I came back to live in the vysotka, which had come to seem less ostentatious. My sisters had been given other apartments to live in with their respective families. The atmosphere is considerably more relaxed. All the people who used to scare me when I was a child have become harmless little old folks."

Kossytkin scoffs at the nouveaux riche who buy apartments in the vysotka believing they are making a good deal. He thinks the building needs an enormous amount of renovation. In 1996, he finally moved into a two-room apartment on the twenty-second floor, after a swap occasioned by his divorce.

His face brightens when we bring up the subject of the dogs, which, attracted by the tea and cookies, jostle us. They are a family—a father, a mother, and two offspring. The mother once again sprawls indifferently on the sofa.

"We initially acquired Prokhar—the father—in 1996. He had been abandoned. It was an especially difficult time for Russians, and thousands of animals were thrown out onto the streets, even purebreds. We bought Tzarina-Budur—the mother—and then came Pulka and Peterhof. Our dogs are of Russian stock, a breed that appeared in the middle of the last century and one of the most beautiful and most pure in the world. All four are great runners. In the warm weather we race them in a stadium

north of Moscow, but when it freezes we don't go, though supposedly the dogs can go outside when it's as low as ten degrees.
We also take a break in midsummer because the heat is bad for
their hearts. The father is old now, but he received a silver
medal at the Russian championship. And Pulka was a three-
time national champion.

"Greyhound racing started shortly after the collapse of
the Soviet Union. Last summer, I went as far as Münster, in
Westphalia [Germany], to participate in the world championship.
That was the first time I had ever been abroad. We made the
trip from Moscow by car with the dogs."

He proudly shows me a photo of the "champions," father
and daughter—in the illustrated magazine *Cat and Dog*, many
copies of which are piled up on a corner of his desk next to his
paintbrushes. Hearing that we are talking about the dogs,
Anya, Kossytkin's wife, is emboldened to join us at the table.

"At Münster," Kossytkin continues, "we were a little disappointed that they didn't win any gold medals—they won a
bronze and a cash prize—but, after a three-day car trip, it's
understandable that they were not in top form. Our car was so
old that we weren't allowed to drive on the German autobahn,
which made the trip even longer.

"I didn't really like Germany, but the people there live
well. Germans are rather nice, even though they are mostly
closemouthed about their problems. Their dogs were better
prepared than ours, which had never run on either a sand or
pavement track before—they only know grass and snow. The
sand got into their eyes and blinded them. I didn't recognize
my animals. They stopped running. It was over before it started.
On top of that, they refused to eat in the car and didn't start to

get acclimated until the second day, when we were about to leave.

"African greyhounds sometimes reach speeds of fifty-five miles per hour, but the Russian borzois only reach about forty miles per hour. They know perfectly well that racing is only a game. On the other hand, they take hunting very seriously, but only when accompanied by horses. There are more and more borzois in Russia—around six hundred in the city of Moscow alone. They are very affectionate animals and not aggressive toward people. We put muzzles on them so they won't fight among themselves, especially the two males.

"That one [he points at Pulka] is a real fighter. I can feel her joy when she beats her adversary. Sometimes she'll bark in satisfaction and excitement. But she doesn't like to run alone. It's too easy and bores her. I remember during one race she was far ahead and then simply stopped to wait for the others. She's only two and a half years old and can race until she's five. Her mother is six years old and her father ten. He hardly moves anymore. The life expectancy of a greyhound is ten years. They have tiny hearts and they're very fragile. All they need is to walk and eat dog food three times per day. They are very impatient and as regular as clockwork. I buy about fifty pounds of meat per week from a butcher who gives me a discounted price. You have to recognize that these dogs take up all of our free time. Not to mention all the space in the apartment."

Anya finally speaks: "For me, it is not a problem of space, but of hands. I only have two! And I cannot walk them all the time, like my husband. They pull too hard!"

Her husband has the last word for both of them:

"If Moscow didn't 'nourish' me, I would have left this

damned city a long time ago and taken my dogs to the country. People don't like the grass and sky. I find this amazing. I even have to force our sixteen-year-old daughter to go walking in the forest with me. When I try to make her appreciate the harmony of nature, she says that she's tired."

CHAPTER 11

Felix is the great-grandnephew of the much feared and hated Felix Dzerjinsky who was the founder of what eventually became the KGB. A ruthless Bolshevik ideologue passionately loyal to Lenin's revolutionary principles, he established the security services to preserve these principles. A huge statue of Dzerjinsky that stood in front of KGB headquarters in Moscow was dismantled by popular demand shortly after the fall of Communism.

Felix and Antonina, fifty-four and about forty-five, respectively, are seated on simple wooden chairs facing each other, hands resting on a table on which sits a crocheted doily. She is made up as if prepared for some formal affair, and her puffed-up hairstyle resembles that of the French singer Muriel Mathieu, who is still very popular in Russia. Antonina keeps turning her head left and right as if to show off her hairstyle to the best advantage. Felix is close-shaven and wears a checkered shirt and dark, frayed suit, which is a little bit tight. His face is open, his hands large and round.

Felix has a low, resounding voice, a little like that of Henry Kissinger, and slow manner of speech. He reminisces about the days when things didn't cost so much. In 1973, during the "stagnation" under Brezhnev, Felix paid only 550 rubles for the very first model of the Jhigouli luxury automobile.

"Today, it costs one hundred and ten thousand rubles [$4,000] minimum," he laments.

"I grew up in a one-room *kommunalka,* of which there were six in Wing A [reserved for employees of the security services]. It was my grandmother, Dzerjinsky's niece, who received the residence permit. We didn't move to this floor of the central section until much later, in 1964, and I haven't moved since. Our neighbor in the communal apartment where we spent fifteen years was a border guard, but he didn't seem to work. His wife sometimes denied us access to the kitchen, or she prevented me from performing my piano exercises because she said that it bothered her. The piano once belonged to Dzerjinsky's sister."

He points at some unframed black-and-white photos neatly arranged against the back panel of the wooden bookcase.

"Here is my mother and my grandmother, her mother, who was Dzerjinsky's sister, and my father . . . and this is my young son, who died here in the courtyard, playing with bottles filled with explosives. One of them blew up in his face. It took a long time for the ambulance to come, so I rushed him to the hospital myself in my Jhigouli. But it wasn't fast enough—he lost too much blood. He died in front of me.

"I was born here and I will die here. I have traveled in forty-six countries as an acrobat and juggler. My father was an artist from Rostov-on-Don. My mother was an engineer with a degree in geography and cartography. I didn't have much choice about my career—it was either the 'organs' [security services] or the circus. Because of my name some people tried to force me to join the 'organs.' One even wanted to make me a general, but I chose the freedom of the artist. When my mother needed something, like a car or pieces of furniture, she wrote to the Party or the government, mentioning that she was the grandniece of Felix Dzerjinsky. That's how she got this apartment. It was even easier during the lifetime of my grandmother Sophie Sigmondova. We rode around in her father's Moskvitch and went to visit him, which she wrote about in a famous letter."

"Turn off the light, please, Felix," interrupts Antonina.

Felix rises heavily and presses the wall light switch. Then he picks up the telephone handset, which rests on a white neoclassical wooden stand, and calls his mother at work.

"At eighty-two years of age, my mother still works. She earns her pin money, but she really does it because she adores being with people, She keeps everything in good order at the House of Composers. I don't know exactly what she does there. She and Grandmother lived in the Kremlin at first; then, in 1948, the year I was born, we found ourselves in this vysotka."

"Here's a picture of Felix's mother," says Antonina. "That's his twin sister, who died last year in an automobile accident."

We are interrupted by the mewing of cats, which press themselves against the legs of the table, their tails curled like umbrella handles. One of them leaps up onto the bedcover, which is made of candy pink synthetic fabric, while the other scratches the side of the upright piano. The bed, awkwardly positioned in a corner of the room, is too large for the space, and the door cannot be closed.

"There was only one cat," said Felix. "Now there are two, Persians. Wait; I'll turn on the lights again. You can't see anything here!"

"No, no, not during the daytime," Antonina insists.

He gives up and goes back to looking at the photographs.

"And here is Dzerjinsky's father," continues Antonina, "a politician. They were Polish—"

Felix interrupts. "Were you in Moscow when they dismantled his statue, on August 24, 1991?" he asks me. "And do you know where the statue is now? At the main House of Artists, with all the others. I recently got a call from Minsk. A group of revolutionaries wanted me to go there and give a lecture about Felix Dzerjinsky. What could I have told them? I wasn't even alive at that time."

"My Felix's mother saved this album," says Antonina. "It was handed down to her from her mother. If I weren't here, Felix would have thrown it away long ago. He doesn't give a damn."

"I already have enough of my own photographs," Felix replies defensively. "All that stuff is useless. These stories don't interest anyone anymore. My grandmother saved everything. She gave lectures about her uncle in schools and corresponded with students on the subject, telling them how he had held her on his knees. I believe everything that she told me about him, since she actually knew him a little, but not what you hear on the television or in the media. The truth is that Felix Dzerjinsky was a man. That's the truth. All he wanted was for everyone to live as well as they could. Today you practically have to steal to become the owner of an apartment."

Antonina turns the yellowed, torn pages of the album. "And here, that's Dzerjinsky in his coffin. On the left is a memorial poem written by your grandmother."

She starts to read but has trouble deciphering the writing.

" 'You sleep from now on, I remember the days'—"

Felix interrupts her: "I've never even read it." He looks contemptuously at the album that his wife has saved with such devotion. "The last time I went to his grave, I was astonished to see that there were no flowers, while Stalin's, right beside it, was covered with them, even though Stalin sent so many people to the camps! He killed so many, right? Every time we visit the tomb of my ancestor, the Kremlin guards make sure we have not forgotten our bouquet. 'Good, good. Very well, pass,'" he says sarcastically, imitating their rural peasant accents.

"The other day, my wife even took an Italian admirer of Dzerjinsky there without me. This Italian knew more about the history of our country than our own students. They let him in without a problem. That tells you something about how the Kremlin is guarded these days."

"I'm not like Felix," says Antonina. "I like history. Dzerjinsky was not a simple man. He has become part of history."

While she is talking, Felix disappears into the next room. He returns carrying a small green bag, out of which he pulls some documents encased in plastic pouches.

"Great. I can't find anything worthwhile in this damned sack. We have to get rid of all these papers. Ah, here is my mother's diploma. When I was little, my father was away most of the time—up to three long months at a time. He was a juggler, acrobat, and magician. He had hands of gold. At least, that's how everyone remembers him. And on top of that, in his spare time he did card tricks. Here, look at this radio in the hallway."

He shows me a miniature wooden cottage with a concealed radio transmitter. He turns a button, and it works perfectly.

"This was his idea, and the frame of that mirror, that's his, too!"

We take a tour of the apartment. Felix proudly lists the purchases he brought back from distant countries, all "friends" of the Soviet Union.

"I remember my first trip to Vietnam and Laos in 1969. At the time we were entitled to a certain amount of pocket money each day. I filmed everything with a real movie camera because video cameras didn't exist yet. When we got home, we projected these films onto white walls. Ah, the flowers of Kuala Lumpur! They greeted us with cheers, we artists of the great Soviet Union! Then it was on to Sardinia, Rome, Tunis, Algeria, Morocco, Mozambique, Angola, socialist Yemen. I was in Turkey twice, Australia, Czechoslovakia, Spain, but never to either Germany or England. In Cuba, Raoul Castro offered me a shirt like his—sky blue, not pink like the others. And Fidel, god, could he speak! He could go on for hours, and without a text. The circus was definitely much more interesting than working in an office."

He shows me some torches sculpted in wood by his father. Their bedroom is freezing. They don't sleep there for the time being because they just bought a new mattress and it hasn't yet been delivered. A lamp is set atop a tall sculpted base. Pictures of dancing gypsies and landscapes hang in the kitchen. In fact, they hang everywhere, even on the bathroom ceiling and walls. Some of the friezes and scenery are pretty well done, if not well placed.

"He was an uncommon man, really gifted," says Antonina with obvious admiration from the kitchen.

"He died about ten years ago, right after my son. Antonina

is my second wife. We've been married only three years."

He lowers his voice even further so she won't hear.

"I had my son with my first wife. I have always been at peace with my family name. When they hear it, most people treat me with a certain respect. Yes, I know that my grandfather founded the Cheka, that he ordered the executions of many people, and that some people consider him a criminal. But today, all you have to do is turn on the television to realize how much criminality there is in our country. In the old days, they didn't fool around with criminals. Dzerjinsky found out who they were and punished them. Today, everybody knows who they are and nobody does anything about it. It's shameful!"

Antonina joins us. "Dzerjinsky adored children and looked after thousands of homeless kids. Look at where we are today! What a horror! A friend told me that in her youth she became acquainted with a boy from Turkmenistan who became an academic. He had come from one of these youth homes Dzerjinsky set up. The Soviet state helped him get an education in Moscow. Most of these kids became professors. Well, every time this professor passed through Moscow, he placed a flower on Dzerjinsky's tomb."

"His name still scares people because he ran the Che-Ka," says Felix. *Che-Ka*. These two letters of the Russian alphabet crack off the end of his circus tongue like a whip on the rump of a horse. ". . . which became the KGB, and now the FSB—as if that changed anything. Of course not! Nothing changed, and the same people work there."

"Before, there was order," adds Antonina. "Today there is absolute disorder. Just look around! Especially at young people! All these kids who hang around in the streets! They could still make something of their lives, but nobody helps them. None of that existed before perestroika. They're all from the capitals of the former Soviet republics."

"Yes, because all around us, there is war—in Moldova, in Central Asia."

We are interrupted when a clock mounted on the wall strikes midnight. The apparently inexhaustible couple returns to the subject of the statue.

"Nowhere else in the world have statues of major historical figures been knocked down," says Felix.

"It wasn't in the way of anybody on [Lubyanka] Plaza."

"I understand that people wanted to sweep away the past, including the KGB. But it has survived. In fact, it is one of the few remnants of the past still around."

"Sometimes in films you still see a portrait of Dzerjinsky," says Antonina dreamily. "The other day, I went to the police station and his picture was hanging on the wall."

"It couldn't have been the police station in this district, because there's a portrait of Willy Tokarev hanging on their wall." Felix snickers.

"That's only because Tokarev was smart enough to give them a poster when he went there to register."

"The life that my father led fascinated me. As a teenager, I decided to become just like him, and I trained for four years at the circus school. I didn't go right into the circus, because my father wanted me to become an artist in theatrical variety shows—to perform in the culture centers, schools, or different institutes. Becoming a circus artist meant never seeing them, always being off on tour. I sent my salary to my mother, who approved my choosing the stage. Sometimes my father came up with acts and we performed them together. For example, one of these numbers was called . . ."

"'The Russian Teapot'!" exclaims Antonina.

"Yes, that's it! 'The Russian Teapot.' We had to juggle with a samovar and some teapots, and then add more and more cups."

He gets up and goes back to the cabinet, from which he removes a gigantic teapot made of orange papier-mâché and covered with white polka dots. With increasing difficulty he also pulls out a number of cups and saucers.

"He also invented an act involving a samovar. I was more of an acrobat-gymnast."

He sighs.

"This is what I did with my life until 1993, when I retired. I never performed in Paris, but four years ago I finally went there as a tourist, in a Mercedes with a Russian friend, an oil magnate who lives in Brussels.

"I often thought about immigrating to the United States. I had a friend there, also a circus artist, who just died. He wanted me to go and become a computer operator like him."

"Felix, call your mother. She must have gotten there by now. Old people are very punctual. I worked all my life as a researcher at the Institute of Industrial Textiles, specializing in synthetic rubber."

"Today, Tonya doesn't have a job. And she types marvelously on the computer!"

He goes off to call his mother.

"I'm Felix's second wife, but we've known each other since we were eighteen. We met at a friend's house. My family also lived in a Stalinist building, not far from Izmailovo Park. I don't go looking for work because in Russia today they only hire people under forty. I don't have a chance. So I twiddle my thumbs."

Felix returns. "I wish my mother would slow down a little and stop working. Yes, yes, she just arrived and will call me back in a minute."

At that very moment, the phone rings stridently.

"Hello, Mama! . . . How are you? . . . Are you at work? . . . Your colleague is sick and you're filling in for him? . . . I wanted to ask you something. Was I born after we were settled in the *kommunalka*? . . . We got this room in which year? . . . In 1947? . . . OK, fine. Here's Antonina. . . ."

"It's always me who has to do everything," says Antonina, sounding aggrieved. But she gets up and goes to the telephone.

"Your mother was given that room," she says when she returns, "and not an apartment, because all the individual apartments had already been allocated."

"That, it's a shell brought back from Cuba," says Felix, pointing. "Impossible to find anything like it in the Crimea. I was also in the Seychelle Islands, where I could tell there was real Communism. No army, no police, free school as well as research. A wonderful country! Nothing else to do all day long except dance the *lambada* and laze on the beach."

"Felix, please turn off the light."

"Of course, there are no museums, no tomb of Napoléon, like in France. Well, I took a photo next to his tomb in the Invalides with my friend the current Russian ambassador to Israel. We met each other in this vysotka, where his parents lived. His father was a KGB general."

Felix continues to flip through the photo albums.

"This other buddy is the Russian ambassador in Iraq today. I wonder what he'll do if the Americans start to bomb. Probably burrow into a cellar! I've heard their salaries double in case of war!"

He bursts out laughing.

"My friend the petroleum magnate who lives in Belgium also grew up in this vysotka."

"Felix's mother lives alone today in her twin sister's apartment. She lived here until Felix's first wife threw her out."

"On the centenary of Felix Dzerjinsky's birth, the authorities had the good sense to offer me an apartment on the eighth floor of this central section, identical to this apartment, but two floors up. I registered there with my first wife. Not wanting to let my mother live alone on the sixth floor, I was forced to deregister the upper floor and to reregister down here. I didn't want to lose the lower apartment in case my mother suddenly died. While all that was happening, my first wife privatized that eighth-floor apartment behind my back, sold it, and pocketed the money. It was possible to do that in those days. My mistake was not to have gotten personally involved in the privatization process. But she made one hundred and forty thousand dollars all the same, and I knew nothing about it for a year!"

Antonina remains silent, her head lowered.

"Imagine my shock when I tried to open the door of the eighth-floor apartment one day and noticed that another family had moved in!"

"Irina—Felix's first wife—explained to him and his mother that while the eighth-floor apartment was being renovated she would come to live with them on the sixth floor for a while.

After four months, Felix's mother pointed out that it was taking a little long. In fact, Irina had tricked them—the apartment had already been sold."

"When this scandal blew up, that was it. In a rage, my ex-wife cleared this sixth-floor apartment of everything worth anything—the television set, the video recorder, the audio system, the washing machine, curtains, bed linens, crockery. She didn't miss a thing! I just let her. She even took the *stenka* [credenza], which my father bought decades ago."

"When I came to live here with Felix, he didn't have anything."

"But the worst part is that before she left, my ex-wife had the unmitigated gall to register our eldest daughter in this sixth-floor apartment where I currently live with Tonya, obviously with the intention of inheriting it—"

"—while Irina had already bought another apartment, where she lives quietly with the money from the sale of the eighth-floor apartment!"

"And then Irina sent my daughter to England without telling me. From England, they called my friend in Belgium to ask him for a thirty-five-thousand-dollar loan on my behalf. I knew nothing about it, of course. It was only a year later, while I was sitting in a restaurant in Moscow with my friend, that he admitted that he had sent money to my wife. I was dumbfounded."

"She is what they call a con artist. Later on, she nearly managed to wrangle another thirty-seven-thousand dollars from our Belgian friend. Today, she's back in Russia and we don't know what she is up to."

"I don't have any more contact with my daughter. She never calls me."

"Felix always had strained relations with his wife. She used to beat him when she drank. Once, she even bit him! When we met each other, around the time his wife was leaving for England, Felix was quite simply scared to death."

They both sigh and are silent for a moment.

"The most important thing is that when I die Antonina should inherit this apartment, not those two people who had so much fun making me suffer."

A few days later, at the same table, I sit with Felix's mother. She leans over the old albums of warping photos, peeling off yellowed newspaper articles stuck to the back of the album.

"These albums were all put together by my own mother. I have a cupboard full of them. I cried so much when they took down the statue from its pedestal. It's Luzhkov's idea. Somebody scrawled the word *executioner* on the statue. But he was an extraordinarily good man who had done nothing except follow the orders of his boss, Lenin."

"He didn't kill anybody!" adds Antonina.

"Well, even if he did shoot a certain number of people, he was only obeying orders." She coughs slightly, then tells me what she does for a living. "I've run the coatroom in the House of Composers since 1962, when I retired. As for the room in the *kommunalka* that we were given in 1947, it was because of my mother, who worked in a military installation. However, she never lived there. She was in prison then, and ended her life in internal exile in the Moscow region. She had been arrested in

1947 on the orders of the NKVD because she was a member of Felix Dzerjinsky's family. She was considered a 'socially dangerous element.' After her death, my sister and I found ourselves alone at the age of sixteen.

"Our name did not help us. Nobody wanted to hire us, no matter what the job. My life was hard in that *kommunalka* without gas, heated by a wood stove. I may be a Communist, but I am not malicious. I respect others."

CHAPTER 12

The outline of a legend of Russian cinema appears in the doorway. In her leather pants and a black wool vest, Klara Luchko makes an impression. Her hair is short and blond, her face smooth and skillfully made up. When she sits on the pink leather sofa, which stands out against the yellowish-orange wall, her legs seem to be even longer. The plush carpet is pistachio green. Stills from her films are everywhere; she is always a femme fatale—fashionable, smiling, her ubiquitous hat worn with elegance and distinction.

Her entire apartment is really a museum, a showcase of the innumerable gifts given her over the course of years by adoring fans. In the second room, which serves as a living and dining room, the television stays on during our entire conversation. In fact, there's a small television in every room. A plate of a stylized woman's face, signed by Picasso, is mounted on top of a cupboard. *"This woman's face resembles yours,"* the painter was said to have commented when giving it to her. Another paneled wall bears a plaque signed by Fernand Léger, presented to her at the Cannes Film Festival of 1955. The bedroom is plainer, all paneled. The kitchen is like one you might find in a mountain chalet—"the opposite of a modern

111

interior," she says proudly—and lined with blue-and-white Gjel porcelain, named after the factory in the Moscow region that produces them.

"Still more gifts," she whispers. "My daughter wishes that I would throw out most of these old things, but I just can't do it."

Klara Luchko has appeared in hundreds of postwar films. Some of them—*The Cossacks of Kuban, The Miners of Donetz, The Young Guard,* and *The Twelfth Night*—were pure Soviet propaganda. They have lots of singing and dancing. Her face is known in all corners of the former Soviet empire: the broad smile, high forehead, and prominent cheekbones have illuminated the movie screen for decades. Her recently published memoirs contain a skillful mixture of youthful and more recent photos. "Luchko doesn't change," "Luchko stays the same," "One forgets her age," read the captions.

"I came from Poltava, a remote Cossack province in Ukraine. My surname comes from the word *luk,* which means 'onion.' My Cossack roles made me famous. *The Cossacks of Kuban* was filmed near my home, and *The Gypsy* is about a Cossack from the Don River region.

"After my parents died, I came up to Moscow to study theater. That's when I rented a small room. Life was hard. Everything changed with *The Cossacks of Kuban,* my first success. In 1955, at the Cannes Film Festival, I made the acquaintance of Fernand Léger and Picasso. I married a well-known artist fifteen years older than me, whom I met during the filming of *Kuban.* We had a daughter.

"The three of us lived in one room of a nine-room *kommunalka* on Kaltchanov Road. Life wasn't easy, but we were young. We lived in our own world. So many things were less important. It was there that one night I had a dream that we were going to be given our own furnished apartment in a special house. That same day, at my dressmaker's, I heard a customer tell him that she had just received an order to move into the new Stalinist skyscraper on Ironmongers Quay. I had never ventured to this side of Moscow before, and I wasn't even aware that the building was under construction. Then this client started talking about how her kitchen was equipped, and it was just like in my dream! I decided to go see this place. Sure enough, right on the embankment, an immense concrete structure was rising, with a central tower that was still under construction.

"A few days later, we heard that we, too, would be given an apartment in this building. My husband and I hurried over to see it. It was the apartment of my dreams, a magnificent two-room space on the fourth floor, with a view of the Kremlin and the Moscow River. The downstairs entrance hall was so vast that my daughter learned how to ride a bicycle in it! Life was beautiful. We frequented the best addresses in the district; we chose from among the best products at the Gastronome. We were like an island of intellectuals and artists with no interest at all in politics. How could the great actor Jarov or the towering poet Yevtushenko even be interested in politics? In winter, I watched people ice-skating on the terrace above the garages. We felt at home here, among our own kind. We were all friendly with one another; we helped one another out; visited one another's homes. It was only much later, in 1963, thanks to the then minister of culture, Ekaterina Fourtseva, that we moved into this three-room on the seventh floor of the central section where the view is even more magnificent. When I am in a bad mood, I sit myself down in the kitchen and admire the gilded cupolas of the Cathedral of Christ Savior. It makes me think of the Taj Mahal, in India.

"Who didn't live in this house! Galina Ulanova, the world-famous dancer, Irina Bugrimova, the lion tamer, writers, actresses, composers, politicians. After the death of Ulanova, there was some discussion about turning her apartment into a museum, an idea that particularly displeased me because I know that Galina would have wanted it to continue to be filled with lively people, not objects. Her dream was that it become a residence for dancers passing through Moscow, so that they didn't need to stay at a hotel. As a museum, it will attract at most five visitors per month. Is that really worth it?

"The actress Faina Ranevskaya also lived here—a real theater legend, which preserved all her unforgettable remarks. Everyone wanted to be her friend, but she ended her life quite alone. She often sat on one of the benches close to the main entrance of the vysotka and waited for someone she knew to pass by. When I arrived, I'd hear her murmur, 'Klara, I want to tell you, you know that role I played so long ago—eh, well, I should have played it differently.' Bugrimova also spent long hours sitting on the bench. Soon I think it will be my turn to sit there and rerun the film of my life.

"My husband died a year after we moved to this apartment. Times had changed. All the papers denigrated this building, claiming that only KGB operatives lived here, that the architecture was dreadful, that it perverted Moscow. Under Khruschev, people were so incensed by the life of Stalin that this building became the object of sarcasm and criticism.

"Some days, I am surprised to find myself dreaming about

an apartment in a newer building, which would undoubtedly be more comfortable and practical. But just the idea of moving horrifies me. Though the air in this neighborhood is particularly polluted because the traffic has increased tenfold during the last decade—I realized it when I walked my dog, which was stolen from me—I've decided to stay here.

"Everything is different now. The kinds of residents who live in the vysotka have changed in proportion to the changes in life itself. Artists, lecturers, composers, and writers who were at the height of their glory in 1952 are no more. Their children are married, and the next generation is different. A second wave of intellectuals and artists arrived in the sixties, bringing us the actress Ludmilla [Lidia] Smirnova, the Yevtushenkos, and the Voznesenskys, but, lately, since the start of perestroika, everything has become lax and we find ourselves under a different regime. All that we knew has been swallowed up in the limbo of the past. People have gone back to detesting us—the residents of this house."

Klara Luchko's daughter, forty-five years old, arrives and fills in more of the story:

"I was born in this building and have lived here for a long time, but when I come back here now I don't recognize anybody. When I was little, everything was neat and the staff of the house always washing the floor and marble walls. It was a real baroque building in the Stalinist rococo style, with sofas, vases, and mirrors in all the public areas. There was a children's playground, a library, a rose garden on the spot where the paid parking lot is today, and a taxi stand. My father planted one of the poplars on the embankment.

"Everything started to fall apart with perestroika. The

monthly charges for the garage are constantly going up. Did you know that on the fifth-floor landing, the whole floor is marble and not parquet? There was a rumor that Stalin was coming to visit the work site. Nobody knew which part of the building he would visit, so an engineer decided randomly that he would cover the landing of the fifth floor of every entrance in marble. Today, I don't like this vysotka. The apartments are out of style, too small, and inconveniently located, but it makes me feel bad to see it deteriorate so quickly."

"In any case," her mother picks up, "these days seem to be more favorable for our building again, because, oddly enough, everything Stalinist is back in fashion. Our vysotka has even been classified—which still didn't stop me from installing air-conditioning in my apartment, though I didn't have the right to modify the building's facade. Luckily, our chief engineer, who knows the house well, came up with the idea of using the technical services level for this purpose. By chance, it's located directly above mine.

"After perestroika, more and more of the retirees had to sell or rent out their apartments. In the courtyard, there's a constant ballet of young bodyguards at the wheels of gleaming black Mercedeses with tinted windows who accompany their 'bosses' right up to their apartments. Some of them have apparently installed Jacuzzis in their bathrooms!"

Klara Luchko tells me that recently in a chic restaurant a table of "new Russians" recognized her and started to applaud. One of them even rose to embrace her.

"Mine is a public profession. What's more, a whole generation grew up on my films, which have become classics. Today, they continue to show children *The Gypsy* and *The Cossacks of*

Kuban in new video versions. One morning I needed an electrician to come to the house, and I received him in a bathrobe. As I accompanied him back to the threshold, he asked if he could hug me. He said, 'You know, usually, when I see you on the screen, you're wearing a hat. That's part of your style. But I like you much more the way you are this morning!'"

She still laughs at it, adding that it's true, that she really likes hats. She has more than a hundred of them.

"I remarried, to a former editor-in-chief of the newspaper *Izvestya,* who became first deputy director of Goskompetchat [Committee of the Press]. Today, he directs an organization that cares for disadvantaged children. He owns a two-room in the center, but I preferred to remain here, so he moved in here and for the time being my daughter occupies his two-room. In my private life, I've had many opportunities. My husbands always understood and accepted me as I am—away most of the time, on tour or visiting abroad.

"In certain rare years, when I was offered roles that I thought were bad, I refused to do them and didn't go on tour. But after perestroika, Russian cinema began to die. It ceased to be national, and state funding evaporated. The film industry used so-called directors, only capable of pronouncing the words 'cut' and 'action,' to launder money. The public turned to television instead. Most of the movie theaters were sold off or turned into furniture or automobile showrooms. Today, in Moscow, the rooms worthy of the name 'cinema'—with Dolby stereo and comfortable seats—show almost exclusively action films and foreign war films. In the provinces, the cinemas are empty. They make money by organizing exhibits. It has become more profitable to make a film for television—like the one I am in the process of shooting now—than for the cinema, but at least you know that the audiences in the provinces will see it. None of the films I've appeared in for the last few years were shown in a movie theater. They are all films for television.

"Why aren't there more women movie stars today? Because the leading roles are always for men. We have very good actresses, but they only get roles as prostitutes or idiots. I hope it's only temporary. However, the more successful new screenwriters find money abroad, and this shows. They make films about our life such as it is, without necessarily involving the mafia or murders. I would advise Goskino to finance screenplays by holding a contest, but the people who run that film bureaucracy lack audacity and effectiveness."

She starts to comment one by one on the stills from *Shaft of Sunlight*, a telefilm that she is currently shooting in Sevastopol and which, apparently, is keeping her amused. She plays the role of a superwoman with ice in her veins, capable of killing. She's been told that the film might be shown in a Moscow theater.

"Very recently, I hailed a taxi on the street. When I got in, I noticed that the driver was very handsome, with superb eyes, dressed very elegantly. When we got stuck in a traffic jam, I tried to engage him in conversation but was dumbfounded when he would hardly answer me. When we arrived at the door of my building, I asked him how much I owed him. Finally he opened his mouth to excuse himself.

" 'I couldn't really answer you because I was afraid you would recognize my Chechen accent and immediately get out of my car,' he stammered. 'I simply want you to know that not all

Chechens are terrorists and criminals, though some here in Moscow would have you believe that!' Surprised and moved, I took one of my pictures from my bag and asked what his wife's name was. 'I am not married,' he said. So I inscribed it to his mother. The man was nearly overcome with gratitude and close to tears. Because of him, I understood the misery of the Chechen people. That was two months ago, and the war goes on. Someone asked me to consider a wonderful screenplay about Chechnya, but as soon as the bureaucrats and the state committee for cinema found out about the subject, they refused to finance us without even glancing at it!"

She describes the scenario in minute detail. It is a melodrama that involved two mothers, a Russian—whom she would play—trying to free her son who has been taken hostage in the blood-soaked, war-torn Caucasian republic, and a Chechen mother of one of the Russian woman's son's jailers. The two women understand each other and try to do what they can for each other, despite the war dragging on between the independence rebels and the Russian forces enlisted to fight them.

"I adore this film project, which celebrates the triumph of humanity over brutality. I would be perfect for the role of the Russian mother, but nobody will give us the funding. We've already appealed to the wealthy Chechens living in Moscow who promised to help us but haven't done anything. The filmmaker Andrei Konchalovsky is currently shooting a film about a psychiatric asylum in Grozny [capital of Chechnya], and using some of the patients as actors, but he probably got American money to do it. It is very hard to find producers here. Chechnya remains a taboo topic, which is so because making a film like this could humanize the conflict. Ending the war is like going on a diet. Here, the hardest thing is to start losing weight. There, the hardest thing is to stop."

CHAPTER 13

Standing straight as an arrow, dressed completely in black, Raisa Struchkova carries herself with all the poise you'd expect of a prima ballerina. Soloist with the Bolshoi Theater from 1944 until 1978, she is now quite elderly, and her voice wavers. She wears bright red lipstick, and her hair is sleek and nicely styled. She glides around her apartment on the tips of her toes, a result of her former profession, no doubt.

Here as well the walls of the apartment have been transformed into photograph galleries of an entire lifetime. Her images show her moving here and there, turning back toward the camera, always gay and smiling, as if ready to leap and whirl into your arms. The serious-looking face of her husband, also a dancer, is in every picture.

More than twenty years after the loss of her husband, Raisa Struchkova still speaks of him with passion. She had wanted to have a child with him—a rare desire for ballerinas, who were advised to concentrate on their career and suppress any maternal instincts. Sitting on her chair, sipping her tea, the aging star gently taps her foot to an imaginary beat.

"I come from a modest family in Saint Petersburg that had no ties to dancing. At school, everyone called me 'Struchok'

[Clove, which in slang connotes laziness] because of my family name. I won a contest at a dance festival in the early fifties and was given an apartment in another part of the city, quite far away from the center. I had gotten married in 1945 to a dancer named Alexander Lapouri, and we were living with my mother. We asked the authorities if they could possibly place us closer to the Bolshoi, where we both worked. After a year of negotiating, our request was approved.

"My first apartment in this vysotka was a two-room located on the second floor of the central section. I exchanged apartment after apartment until I finally got this four-room, where I've lived for twenty-six years, and where I intend to finish my days.

"At the time—the end of the seventies—there were four of us living here, my husband and I, my mother, and our *niania* [nanny]. My mother died in 1984 and Katya, my *niania*, last year. For my entire adult life I never had to bother with household errands or financial matters. That was the domain of Katya— honesty and righteousness personified. Pure as they come. She was not a *niania* in the usual sense of the term, because she didn't raise me, but she spent her whole life in our service, and I would not have been separated from her for anything.

"We often invited students and actors to our home. I always was afraid they didn't have enough to eat. My husband made fun of me for being more preoccupied with their stomachs than with their musical education, but I knew they were hungry."

She gets lost in this memory. Her voice becomes even shakier, but her eyes burn more brightly. She hasn't forgotten anything.

"I used a little trick. I asked them if they wanted to eat first or to listen to music. I was right. They always rushed over to the sandwiches my mother and Katya had prepared! We also made them listen to recordings of symphony orchestras, American, German, and Italian, which we had bought whenever we had a chance to go abroad. These records were unobtainable in the Soviet Union. They are all still right over there. I haven't touched them since. Then we would start to dance—sometimes fifteen of us—on this parquet floor!

"I met my husband, who had a Georgian father and Russian mother, when I was about ten. During the war, we had been evacuated to the same city on the Volga, where we studied together until 1944. We married a year later. Like me, Alexander was a principal dancer at the Bolshoi. We spent thirty years without ever being apart, not until the day of his accident, six days before his fiftieth birthday.

"He had gone alone to a birthday party that evening. Someone had lent him his car and driver to bring him home. It was summer. A new layer of asphalt had just been laid and it was still burning hot and soft. The car crashed only a few hundred feet from here. The driver suffered from some contusions, but he lived. I could have prosecuted him in court, but what good would that do? I only regret that he didn't come to my husband's funeral.

"Today I teach the theory of classical dance. That makes fifty-six years that I've been with the Bolshoi. I can't do anything else. Times may change, but classical ballet remains, though it does evolve. The Bolshoi maintains numerous contacts with various foreign dance troupes. Techniques and influences multiply. *Swan Lake* was out of fashion six years ago, but today they produce a new, different version, more modern. That's normal. It's the cycle of life. But what saddens me is that the tickets are so expensive. They sometimes give free performances for retirees and orphans, or they invite them to a regularly scheduled show. The public, alas, lacks culture. They sometimes forget to turn off their cell phones.

"In 1981, I agreed to become editor-in-chief of an illustrated magazine called *Soviet Ballet* [renamed *Ballet* in 1991], but not before hesitating, because I didn't know anything about the business and really didn't want the power. But when they said that a person not interested in power would be ideal, I became excited about the job. The editorial staff and the technical support of the newspaper *Izvestia* were very helpful, but this support ended in 1996. After that I was no longer really up to it, and submitted my resignation.

"Galina Ulanova was one of the first to write an article for our magazine. She came from Saint Petersburg, like me. Her father was a director of the Mariinsky Theater, and her mother was a dancer. She was a very sweet woman of great delicacy and a shy, reserved character. She had been granted an apartment in this vysotka in 1952. Her hometown missed her, but Moscow made her a star.

"Ulanova had magnificent feet, which is essential for a dancer. People even called them 'feet that speak'! She was an amazingly lyrical performer, full of emotion, who excelled in *Giselle, Sylphide,* Juliet, as well as in the second and fourth acts of *Swan Lake*. She felt the music and her technique and artistic level were unique. For her, it was necessary, but not enough, to kick the leg as high as possible. It was important not simply to see the flowers in the decor, but to smell their fragrance. That's

what made the difference—about that I was in complete agreement. To her great regret, she felt that this way of approaching
dance was in the process of disappearing.

"I was her understudy more than once. We were very similar. Sometimes we even changed places. One evening when
she danced Giselle, I waited backstage. During the second act,
there was a sudden silence. Rumors began to spread. The
director hurried into my dressing room. Galina had just had a
problem with her leg and they had had to bring down the curtain. I hurriedly put on makeup and my costume and ran onto
the stage. A Chinese delegation was in the audience that evening. Much later, during one of my tours of China, a man
raised his glass in my honor and explained in front of the whole
party that he had seen me in *Giselle* when I replaced Ulanova.

"At only twenty years old I was the fourth Bolshoi ballerina
to dance *Cinderella*. That evening, the entire theater staff
gathered in the wings to cheer me on. Galina offered me the
most beautiful bouquet of flowers I'd ever gotten in my entire
life, and, in place of a fur slipper, a pair of very pretty shoes
that I kept for a long time.

"For us dancers, Galina was our point of reference, our
North Star. She retired at just the right time, which is an art in
itself. That moment should not come too early or too late. I
had no sooner finished my dance training than my professor
said to me, 'Struchok, now is the time you must prepare for
retirement.' I was flabbergasted.

"Nevertheless, the last time I danced *Don Quixote*, Maya
Plissetskaya, who was in the audience, came to tell me that I
had been sublime. I was barely forty years old, but that was the
night I decided to call it quits. It was very exciting. I asked the

staff to find champagne and teacakes. When everyone was there—technicians, makeup staff, dressers, and stagehands—I announced that I had given my last performance.

"Our profession is unforgiving because on the one hand with age we master technique, acquire experience, and attain artistic stature, and on the other hand our bodies deteriorate. You have to be determined to leave the stage. No one should ever dance to the limits of their strength. That, one should never do."

CHAPTER 14

In Galia Yevtushenko's kitchen, we munch on delicious almonds and drink aromatic Italian coffee, which she serves burning hot. Her two-room is charming, tastefully furnished with antiques and objects that mean something special to her. On the walls of the living room are portraits of her—as well as two still lifes by Robert Falk and a landscape by Max Ernst. The man with whom she spent the best years of her life, the poet Yevgeny Yevtushenko, became world-famous during the Khrushchev era. His poem "Babi Yar"—literally, the "Ravine of the Good Woman"—spoke of the unspoken things that were happening in the Soviet Union. Before it, nothing had filtered out about the massacre of Jews that had taken place in Ukraine.

In 1959, accompanied by his compatriot, the poet Voznesensky, the young and brilliant Yevtushenko performed before a packed Albert Hall in London, reading his verses in Russian, a language only a tiny minority of people in the room knew. The two men became the poets of the moment, the new face of Soviet intelligentsia, living proof that Communism could be humanized.

Galia Yevtushenko was the poet's second wife.

"We moved into the twelfth floor of the central section of this miserable building in 1969. Yevtushenko asked me to go see the apartment. I came back very upset. The building was monstrous and the neighborhood both repugnant and impractical without a car. I had no desire to leave our two-room near the Aeroport metro [station], but Yevtushenko was determined to live in this Stalinist vysotka and had organized a swap with the nephew of one of the building's architects. The immense foyer of the new apartment and its 430-square-foot living room had convinced him. He thought it would be the ideal place to hang his paintings. He had at least two hundred. To Yevtushenko, this vysotka was synonymous with prestige. It was as simple as that. It was an 'elite' residence, he said.

"We had two separate telephone lines. Sometimes both got cut off at the same time. Our telephone began to 'malfunction' as soon as I started to associate with the Sakharovs. Our neighbors, the Voznesenskys, had the same 'technical' problem. One morning, Andrey Voznesensky's wife Zoya was so furious when her telephone line went dead that she ran down to the cellar—which was prohibited—pushed open some doors, and attacked the guys who listened to our conversations. There were about thirty of them sitting at consoles, taking notes. Their technique was so primitive that you could tell the exact moment when they started to listen in.

"Sometimes, the lines got all scrambled up. Once, when I picked up the telephone receiver, I stumbled onto a conversation that was so surreal I couldn't keep myself from listening in. It was obviously between a mother and daughter. One of them had just bought a *stenka,* a Soviet status symbol. It was still very important to possess one even though they didn't have the books to put in it. 'Has Grandfather seen it?' one of them asked. 'I don't have a single book; what am I going to fill it with?' the other one complained. 'Go to Sadko [a store reserved for the *nomenklatura*—those with positions of privilege] and buy yourself something,' the first replied. Really, this is a crazy country, difficult to describe. Even Dostoyevsky couldn't make it here!

"I much preferred to live in our dacha in Peredelkino [north of Moscow, where the state had given a small number of writers and artists second homes]. During all our years here I never got to know anybody except my neighbor across the hall, the widow of an admiral and a very nice old woman. A little farther down our hallway, there was a man who bore an uncanny resemblance to Lenin. He wore the same cap. I was always afraid to be alone with him on the elevator! I didn't make peace with this monstrous building until recently, when the bad vibrations that had emanated from it for decades finally dissipated.

"I moved into this two-room in 1992, when my son decided he wanted to live alone. When I sold the apartment on the twelfth floor to Irene Commeau, a Frenchwoman, she found him a two-room and relocated me here in exchange. Irene took care of everything, including the red tape. I left the piano behind for her, as well as a giant china closet, a unique piece that occupied an entire wall and would have been very difficult to remove from the apartment. At the time, I would have definitely settled in Estonia, where I bought a country house much later. Or I would have stayed in France on the invitation of the writer Viktor Nekrassov, with whom we were very friendly.

"Some residents of this monster are monsters themselves.

For example, I have no respect for Bogoslovsky, who hates me back because I never restrained myself from shouting at the top of my lungs that he worked for the KGB. All you have to do is look through the KGB archives published in Paris to confirm that he held the rank of lieutenant colonel. Everyone knew it, and he is undoubtedly collaborating with them to this day. Back then, it was widely known that this building was infested with agents.

"Bogoslovsky took a dislike to me after a reading by Yevtushenko, when I saw him to the door at the end of the evening. We had started to talk about Solzhenitsyn and Maximov, but he wouldn't let us speak about the horrors. In front of my mortified husband, I opened the door, called the elevator, and told Bogoslovsky to leave. That was just after Solzhenitsyn's banishment to the West. Later, when Yevtushenko tried to excuse him, I retorted that this very progressive image that he, Yevtushenko, had given to the West would be appreciated in Russia, too!

"Actually, we fought constantly. Our trips abroad were nothing but a series of scandals. At the heart of our disputes was politics, because we had totally different opinions. I didn't like his poetry, and he knew it. There are many letters—I saved them—in which he accused me of destroying him and of destroying his art. His success was enormous, but extremely fleeting.

"We were married for seventeen years. He was my second—and last—husband. Now he splits his time between the United States, where he teaches courses during the academic year, and Russia, where he comes to rest for the summer. He still keeps a dacha and an apartment in one wing of the Hotel

Ukraine, another Stalin-era skyscraper. In fact, I never was in love with him. My first husband was ten years older than me and was a very jealous man. At the beginning of our affair, Yevtushenko used to recite verses to me from Blok, Pasternak, Akhmatova, Tsvetaeva, and Mandelstam, whom nobody knew then. That's how he seduced me.

"We stopped living together in 1980, and our divorce was finalized in 1983. We fought in court for three years. Ours was the first divorce proceeding in the whole country to be done in public. I almost had to go all the way to the Supreme Soviet, because Yevtushenko balked at providing me with alimony. I was also brought in by the police, because he claimed that I had stolen his paintings. I don't know why our divorce went so badly. One thing is for sure: Bogoslovsky, whom he must have needed at some point so that the KGB would let some of his 'trifles' pass censure, helped to provide evidence against me.

"I am Jewish. When Yevtushenko read me 'Babi Yar'—for which Shostakovich composed his Thirteenth Symphony—I started thinking he was anti-Semitic, because it seemed to me that he had built his whole career on the backs of the Jews. He cried about that. On a trip to Paris, he kept telling everyone proudly that his wife was Jewish. Our relationship became more and more strained. However, we did have three happy days in the United States—at Arthur Miller's house and then with Jacqueline Kennedy."

Turning pensive for a moment, Galia leans over some boxes of photographs. One of them shows Yevtushenko and Picasso, who had just become acquainted, deep in conversation. Galia looks beautiful with her dark hair, heavy bangs cutting across her forehead, and enormous blue eyes so wide-set that they seem to look to the side.

"This was the day I realized that they resembled each other incredibly. A couple of bad characters. Yevtushenko was large, Picasso small. But I hated him at first sight."

In almost every photograph, the real "star," the one all eyes turn to, is Galia, who deliberately looks away.

"My father was a journalist and a member of the writers' union. When I was organizing my files recently, I found his membership card, dated 1934. I was six years old the last time I saw him. He worked in Khabarovsk, in the Far East, as president of the local radio broadcasters' committee. In 1938 he was accused of being a spy for Japan, arrested, and shot. I've never returned to the site of his death in Siberia. It's too far. I don't have the strength to do anything except stay in my bed or get myself to Estonia in the summer. Nothing interests me anymore. However, I did manage to send money to build a tomb in my father's name via the memorial organization that Elena Bonner, Sakharov's widow, founded.

"I used my father's name until my first marriage in 1952, then lost all evidence of my identity. My first husband burned all my identity papers during one of his temper tantrums. We had met in a restaurant. At the time, my mother and my aunt, both Jewish, were in prison. Because my first husband had been a winner of Soviet prizes, I needed him to protect me.

"Alexi Simonov [president of the Glasnost Defense for Journalism] always told me that I came from a family of 'enemies of the people.' But my maternal grandparents had been true Bolsheviks, members of the Social-Democratic Party since it was founded in 1898. My grandfather was Commissioner of the People of Cinema, and his wife served as his assistant. My grandmother was the daughter of a rich Jewish businessman in Siberia who detested the Russians and even disowned my mother when she married a Russian.

"In the fifties, when I wanted to enroll in medical school, I was not admitted because my Jewish nationality was indicated on my passport. Since I had a Russian father, I would have been entitled to have been listed as 'Russian.' I had that right, but I didn't do it."

Galia Yevtushenko changes the subject: "My grandmother once sent me to the market to buy ten pounds of potatoes. I had three thousand rubles in my pocket. These were old rubles, and a pound cost six hundred rubles. That was a lot of money. A gypsy approached me and offered to predict my future. I asked how much it would cost. It was the equivalent of one pound of potatoes! I told myself that my grandmother wouldn't notice if I returned with one less pound. To this day, I remember every word this gypsy told me: 'You will always live a comfortable life but will never fall in love. In fact, you will always be alone.' At the time, this bothered me. Me, so young, so beautiful, never to love? Then, since I wasn't pleased, she demanded seven hundred rubles to alter my fate. Alas—or fortunately—I had already bought the potatoes and didn't have any more money!

"Under the Soviet regime, I never had the impression of lacking freedom. On the contrary, I always felt that it was the only thing I had: I was born free. In 1969, when Bella Akhmadulina—Yevtushenko's first wife—and I were walking down the street a little tipsy, we were reprimanded sharply by some policemen. I asked them if they had no shame about what was going on in Czechoslovakia. They immediately arrested us.

When they read our names on our passports, they couldn't get over it. They had 'nabbed' the two wives—former and current—of the most decorated poet of the time!

"I bought a little house in Estonia at the beginning of perestroika. It is the first place Sakharov went to right after his exile in Gorky. At the time, you bought a visa right at the border. The Estonians have always been nice to me. Some even advised me to put up a sign reading: JEWISH on the wall of my house to show that I wasn't Russian. Today, there are almost more Russians than Estonians in Estonia, and the process to get visas has become very strict.

"Since the early eighties, my life has been affiliated with that of Lucia [Elena Bonner], who now lives in the United States. Their six years of exile seemed to last an eternity. I even wrote a letter to Gorbachev in which I told him why I felt contempt for him. On the other hand, I knelt before him for having freed Sakharov. Why aren't the intellectuals speaking out about what's going on in Chechnya? If Sakharov were still alive, this carnage would have been stopped long ago. In Putin's Russia, the threat of prison hovers over everyone."

THE COCKROACHES

(BY YEVGENY YEVTUSHENKO)

Cockroaches in the skyscraper—
God has not spared us.
Nor has the Moscow City Council.
Tragic panic all around, excepting for
The cockroaches who are staging their attack.
Admirals and ballerinas,
The nuclear scientist and the poet,
Burrow under bedclothes.
Roach-refuge? Not to be had!

On my table sits an ode—
Hard labor—
While out of the wastebasket
Visitors swarm.
Zykina starts to sing and—presto!—
From the ceiling
A roach choir chimes in.
The composer Bogoslovsky
Strikes a chord
And onto the keyboard hops
A slippery little reddish devil.

Cockroaches, orderly, omnivorous—
Are archeologists of dirty dishes.
While art-critic cockroaches
Crawl across the pictures on the walls.
O cockroaches, in the luggage of what pious little old lady

Did you make your quiet way
Into our huge domicile
On the banks of the Moscow River?
And, formed by ages past,
Cockroach psychology
Deploys the threats and flatteries
Of those whose modus operandi is:
"Worm your way in!"
Take that boy there:
To hear him, he is a knight,
Ready to give his all for Truth.
Only a certain slickness in him
Tips you off—careful!
Cockroach!
On plagiarists, smacking their mandibles,
On cockroaches got up à la Pouchkine,
Grunting out their verses,
No one is sprinkling insect powder.

And amusement! Entertainment!
An "Oho!" in a restaurant, turned ominous,
Careens through every chink
Onto the public stages.
All the routine stuff, all the gypsy stuff,
The whole kit of warm-hearts-in-the-snowy-vastness—
Tacky cockroach stuff.
The hands that hold the microphone are paws.
Our house needs cleaning out.
It will be a bad thing, comrades,
If our rockets soar into the heavens

With stowaway roaches on board.
Don't spare the powder, then, comrades,
When cockroaches little and big
Have forced their nasty way
Into our skyscraper—
Our socialism.

Translated from the Russian by Donald Fanger.

CHAPTER 15

Galina Arbuzova's stepfather, Constantine Paustovsky (1892–1968), was the author of many articles, poems, short stories, and novels. Toward the end of his life, he wrote a revealing autobiographical work called *History of a Life*.

The famous poet's room in the fifth-floor apartment remains just as it was when he lived there. For Galina, this is a way of preserving her stepfather's memory. There is a simple bed, a couch, a wooden bureau, and all of his books. The walls are apple green. Scraggly plants climb the whitewood arch separating the area reserved for the master from the dining room.

"I haven't added anything except the television and the icons," she says. "My mother and I moved into this apartment with Paustovsky a little after the arrest of Beria. Actually, Stalin never intended to allocate an apartment like this to Paustovsky. He didn't like it when people divorced. My stepfather spoke often about his divorce and openly announced his new marriage to my mother. She also was divorced.

"That year—1953—the interior courtyard looked like a concentration camp, with prisoners, barbed wire, watchtowers, and armed men. Nobody was surprised that these prison camps had been established right in the heart of Moscow, just as Solzhenitsyn described in *The First Circle*."

Vladimir Jelyeznikov interrupts: "A few years ago, when I had surgery on my eye, it turned out that my roommate at the clinic had been one of the former commandants of a prison camp installed on the work site of this building. He told me that Beria adored this vysotka, but that the construction supervisors would not for anything in the world risk going to the upper levels of the structure—for fear of encountering prisoners who would throw them over the side. There were also some cases of suicide here."

"We were also proud that for several decades this vysotka housed the most well known and most powerful shortwave radio jammers in the country," Galina Arbuzova adds sarcastically. "And who knows if it isn't still here! I'm sure that all the equipment is still up there," she points to the upper levels of the central tower, close to the spire, "maybe even modernized.

"The minute we moved in, my mother destroyed the ventilation ducts installed in each room because she suspected that they were hiding microphones. As a result it was always sweltering in our apartment. But 'they' continued to listen in on our telephone conversations. I think that's still the case for certain occupants of the building, particularly foreigners. Their listening system was so primitive that you immediately knew it was happening. Suddenly there would be a long silence with a sort of vibration in the headset.

"Our former cleaning lady worked for the KGB for a long time. We knew all about it. She had to write up reports about our comings and goings, but my mother was of the opinion that it was better to know your enemy. Our cleaning lady also told us about having seen an apartment stuffed full of listening equipment in the first entryway of our wing. She was a simple woman, very kind, who was practically part of our family. She must have known that we knew who she worked for, but we never spoke about it directly. When my parents died and we could no longer afford to pay for the services of a full-time cleaning lady, she still wanted to stay. KGB people never retire. Then she went to work in the Germans' apartment, the first foreigners to settle in our vysotka.

"Five of us lived in this three-room space. Paustovsky had a hard time working here. That's why, until the fall came, he preferred to write at Taroussa, a village outside Moscow. During winter, he holed up in Yalta, where an apartment was reserved for him in the House of Artists. There he mainly wrote articles and texts intended for his students, and he read a lot. When we had guests, the bureaucrats at the House of Writers even called my mother to suggest which waiters and maître d's to use. She invariably refused, knowing that all those guys were from the KGB. In 1958, when the scandal over the foreign publication of *Doctor Zhivago* exploded, Paustovsky wrote to Boris Pasternak to invite him to spend a few quiet months in his house in Taroussa, but Pasternak declined because he didn't feel at home in the countryside.

"Paustovsky never really associated with the *shest-dessyatniki* [designates writers of the sixties, including Vassily Aksionov, Andrey Voznesensky, and Yevgeny Yevtushenko, all three inhabitants of the *vysotk*a on Ironmongers Quay] who belonged to another generation. On the other hand, he knew the poet-singer-bard Bulat Okudjava well. Okudjava was the first to publish in *The Pages of Taroussa*, which contained works Paustovsky collected from authors who neither wanted nor could be published in Moscow under any pretext, not being on 'the right side.' Some became dissidents. Their literary reviews were prohibited and their published works destroyed.

"Paustovsky went abroad in 1962 for the first time, as part of a delegation of cultural figures. They refused to allow my mother to go, but I accompanied him. Andrey Voznesensky and Viktor Nekrassov were also on the voyage. We made a tour of Europe, stopping in different cities, including Paris. Before we left, the Party summoned me to give me advice about 'the manner of my behavior abroad.' They also wanted me to take all sorts of notes about Paustovsky—his habits, his meetings, his friends, his work. I told them that Paustovsky was a genius and that I admired him. They offered me tea and cakes to coerce my cooperation.

"Strangely, Paustovsky had no friends in the vysotka. He only went on one visit, to the actress Faina Ranevskaya, at whose place the poet Anna Akhmatova, whom he knew well, was also staying. He knew perfectly well what kind of people resided here.

"One day he ran in to the composer Nikita Bogoslovsky in the courtyard. They began a conversation. Paustovsky claimed that he was in a hurry, that he had to rush off to a store to buy a radio receiver, which was fairly hard to find in those days. Bogoslovsky told him that he had lots of sets at his place, and offered to sell one to him. Taken aback, my stepfather didn't say either yes or no. When he got home, he declared that he had no intention of having Bogoslovsky's radio in his home, even if it was in very good condition. At that very instant the telephone rang! It was Bogoslovsky, who said he was coming right down to bring the set to us! Deeply embarrassed, Paustovsky didn't even want to see it, but he felt forced to buy the radio, which he never used. My mother liked using it because it worked well. Bogoslovsky had clearly tried to buy the friendship of his famous neighbor.

"When I hear our journalists today claim that nobody knew anything about what was going on under Stalin, I'm disgusted. I knew all about it from the beginning. In our family, we said things out loud that everyone else hardly dared to whisper. I knew, for example, that they had arrested my grandfather even though I was only four years old, because we talked about it at home. He was released thanks to a change of management within the KGB. There was a new wave of arrests in 1945. They simply took the lists of freed ex-prisoners and arrested them again.

"In those days we had very beautiful dogs, Irish setters. During one morning walk, one of them suddenly froze before a sewer drain and wouldn't budge. Finally they pried off the lid, and there, chained to the drainage pipes, were some confused-looking prisoners, among them my grandfather! My grandmother hurried to the headquarters of the GPU. Apparently they did that when there was no more space in the prisons. She was so indignant she even sent a telegram to Stalin.

"I knew about everything. I have a half sister, five years my junior, a daughter from my father's second marriage. My mother put up her ex-husband and his family for a time. We were all crammed into a large room of a *kommunalka* that we divided with a partition. I trained my little sister to keep my secrets. When she was five years old and I was ten, she would sit on a large trunk and I would say to her, 'Varya, repeat after me: Sta-lin is Hit-ler.' She'd say it in a quiet voice and then burst into tears.

"The village of Taroussa, with a population of a hundred, became home to a certain number of dissidents who had been released from the camps but who were prohibited from coming within sixty-five miles of Moscow. To facilitate their surveillance work, the Soviet secret services installed a KGB detachment there. They posted eleven of their agents. This field office still exists. It was never closed, just in case.

"During the seventies, after Paustovsky's death, KGB cars could often be seen hiding at the other end of Taroussa, watching all comings and goings, particularly when friends came over to celebrate his birthday, March 31. One year after his death, two officers even had the gall to show up as mourners. Getting rid of them tactfully was tricky because they had found a good excuse. They've played their little game every year since then. By 1975, I was sick of it. I simply set up a table just for them in an adjoining room, apologizing but stating that we preferred to be among ourselves. This took them by surprise—and they were furious!"

CHAPTER 16

WING V, ENTRYWAY 8, FIFTH FLOOR:
VASSILY AND MAYA AKSIONOV

WING V, ENTRYWAY 4, EIGHTH FLOOR:
ANDREY AND ZOYA VOZNESENSKY

Novelist Vassily Aksionov has lived and taught in the United States since 1980, but after the Soviet regime collapsed he and his wife, Maya, began returning regularly to Russia. He is a member of the jury for the Triumph Literary Prize, directed by the spouse of his colleague and friend Andrey Voznesensky, who also lives in the building.

"Maya lived in this building for a long time with her first husband, the documentary filmmaker Roman Karmen. After he died in 1968, I moved into the apartment with her. But wherever we were, and wherever we went, dangerous revolutionaries that we were, we were constantly followed by the KGB. So we decided to immigrate to the United States in 1980. A friend of Maya moved into our apartment.

"At the beginning of perestroika, officials from the building administration took advantage of our absence to forcibly evict Maya's friend. They just wanted to take the apartment back. After 1991, thanks to the new administration under the liberal Moscow mayor Sergey Stankevitch, we were finally given an apartment that, by a strange coincidence, was right in this same vysotka as our old apartment. We privatized it under the new registration rules, something we couldn't have done with Karmen's apartment.

"This building has no particular significance for me. I'm here almost by accident. When I was young, I detested this imitation-Kremlin architectural style. We used to call it 'pastry style.' In Warsaw, when an almost identical building was erected as a sort of cultural center, the locals called it a 'baker's nightmare.' This type of construction was widely mocked in the sixties."

Aksionov is referring to the Palace of Sciences in Warsaw, designed by Moscow architect Lev Rudnev and donated by the USSR to the Polish people in 1954. To soften the dominating effect of this Soviet work, considered by many Poles to be a reminder of the Stalinist regime, the mayor of Warsaw authorized construction of another skyscraper in the area after the fall of Communism.

"I never would have imagined that one day I would live in a place where one of the windows on the fifth floor carries the inscription *stroily zakluchyony* [built by prisoners]. What an incredible irony that the son of a *zek* lives in a house built by *zeks!*" Vassily Aksionov's mother, the historian Yevgenia Ginzberg, was incarcerated for a long time in the prisons of the Gulag, about which she is one of the main witnesses, in her memoir, *Vertigo*.

"Later on, however, I realized that this vysotka could also become an object of nostalgia. I wrote a lyric about it in *Zolotaya nasha zheliezka* [Our Golden Ironburg: A Novel with Formulae]. Highly respectable men lived in this building—and still do, like the composer Bogoslovsky. One always ate French [cuisine] in his home. He claimed that food was delivered fresh every morning from the Parisian market of Rungis. Later I got to know the poet Yevgeny Yevtushenko, who lived in a luxurious four-room space. I remember one evening when I brought along the German writer Heinrich Böll to his apartment. A sign in the hallway in large red letters attracted Böll's attention. It read: AGIT-PUNKT [propaganda center]. Böll wanted to know what it meant. I told him that the office was a little like a gas station: you went there to fill up the tank when it was low.

"In spite of the years, the feeling of the vysotka remains the same. I call it the *kommandantura* [command center]. In thirty immense floors, the skyscraper embodies the essence of the Soviet saga over the last five decades. Each apartment lays claim to its own distinct destiny. One day I saw an old woman stepping out of a fruit and vegetable shop—a common sight, but in this case it was Irina Bugrimova, the greatest lion tamer of the Soviet circus. This superwoman has become a defenseless little old lady! She's still immensely popular, though.

"Each in their own way, the residents of this vysotka have served the Soviet regime without really meaning to. They were the elite, although that didn't mean the regime didn't spy on them. We were all slaves. Still, there was a difference between the common slaves—the majority of the population—and the elite slaves. Nobody dared to hope for a better way of living than what this building provided. When I lived in a *kommunalka* off Kropotnitsky Road, a line with thirty-five people formed in front of the single toilet in the apartment building every morning! That was typical of life under Stalin."

Maya Aksionova joins the conversation: "I always loved the Taganka neighborhood. I grew up here with my parents in a workers' dormitory. I used to race down these sloping alleys on a bicycle. My first impressions of this monstrous skyscraper are tied to my tumultuous life with Roman Karmen. We were living in his apartment in the VK wing, above the Illusion Cinema, and I was very close to the ballerina Raisa Struchkova. But when I left the Soviet Union in 1979, I lost the right to return. Even when my mother died in 1987, I could not get a visa to attend the funeral."

Zoya Boguslavskaya, energetic and erudite wife of the poet Andrey Voznesensky, runs the Triumph Prize, an "independent" literary award she created in 1992 with help from the wealthy magnate Boris Berezovsky, now living in self-imposed exile in Great Britain. Before that she had been part of the Stalin Prize committee, one of the highest distinctions in the country.

"In 1965, the authorities summoned Andrey to ask whether we were interested in a three-room space of five hundred and twenty-five square feet in an 'old' house—it was already over ten years old—the vysotka on Ironmongers Quay. We were ordered to move into a specific apartment in the entryway of Wing V, on the eighth floor. I knew the premises well because I had already been there to visit the writers Tvardovsky and Paustovsky, and the ballerina Galina Ulanova. In fact, Galia Yevtushenko, who was being given a four-room in this vysotka, let us spend one night in their apartment while it was still empty. My relationship with Andrey was still secret then. When people found out about it, it became such a scandal, because I was a divorced woman with a child. We had to put up with gossip for six months.

"On moving day, we were stunned when someone opened

'our' door, looking perplexed. We showed him the official document that gave us the right to move in. The man, a well-known
academic, was furious! He said that there had to have been a
mistake, that he occupied this apartment and had no intention
of leaving the premises. I dissolved in tears. I already imagined
myself living here. Things weren't resolved until two years
later, but we were finally able to move in. The apartment was
disgustingly filthy. With no money to buy furnishings, we had to
content ourselves with little. Our friends gave us a lamp, a
table, a chair, and some other things. Today, my son, who works
for an American firm, lives here, and we've retired to our
dacha."

Andrey Voznesensky joins the conversation: "Having
trained as an architect, I detested these vysotkas. They look like
monuments. Their Stalinesque feeling bothered me. Nostalgia
for socialist-style architecture was so strong that it became
painful. But I also have to admit that the vysotka is a wonderful
example of its kind. It was well designed by its architect,
Chechulin. I would sometimes drop by the construction site to
take a closer look at it. He made living here pleasant, with these
high ceilings and thick walls.

"One evening, we hosted the American senator McCarthy
[Sen. Eugene McCarthy]. As he was leaving, we couldn't find
his *kalochki* [galoshes] where he had left them beside the door
when he came in. I told him that the concierge must have
taken them to rinse them off, but he had to be careful so that
the next day the newspapers didn't claim that an American senator had gotten so dead drunk at the Voznesenskys' home that
he couldn't even put on his *kalochki!*

"Our elevator used to go up and down at an infuriatingly

slow pace. Another night, we hosted Ted Kennedy and his wife on an official visit to the Soviet Union, accompanied by a correspondent from *Time* magazine. They arrived around two in the morning and left around four in the morning. Escorting them out to the landing, I could clearly see—he didn't even bother to hide himself—a small, husky KGB agent lying in wait for us just outside the door.

"To fill the embarrassing moment of silence after the element of surprise had passed, the agent told us in a solemn voice that the elevator was out of order. I responded coldly that a Soviet elevator worked all the time. I pressed the button to open the doors and we all piled in. But the car didn't budge because there was too much weight. Kennedy's wife said, in English, 'I think there is one too many of us.' Without saying a word, the Chekist stepped out, and the elevator began to move. He must have run down four steps at a time, because he reached the ground floor at the same time we did! It was like in a police film . . . They spied on us all the time and listening devices were planted in the walls.

"These days I don't spend much time at Ironmongers Quay. This apartment was my first real home—for that reason, I love it—but I hardly ever worked here. I used to travel and went out at all hours. Besides, in the sixties I was assigned a room in a dacha in Peredelkino by Littfond [the organization in charge of writers during the Soviet period]. I started making pretty good money from my books. Each edition sold about two hundred thousand copies. That gave me the means to build my own dacha in the huge garden behind the state-owned house. I didn't have the right to build on Littfond property, so in the end, I exchanged the dacha I had just built for the right to live in a neighboring dacha, where I reside to this day. We have made numerous improvements, but it still doesn't belong to us.

"The first time I went abroad was in 1960—to the United States with Yevtushenko. It was the second trip for him. We became very close, until our paths diverged later. On the way back, we gave a reading in London. We read our poems, which had been translated into English. It was a huge success. I have a photograph of a very young Indira Gandhi standing onstage next to us. At Tomsk, in Siberia, I filled a stadium. In Moscow, my readings took place in Luzhniki Stadium! We were extremely popular all over the USSR. In Moscow, my favorite venue was always the Tchaikovsky Conservatory, which could hold two thousand people.

"Today, poetry is not very popular. It's not a medium that corresponds well with our times, but when I do appear in public the room is always packed with sensitive young people who respond to my style of writing. Poetry is nothing more than poetry. It doesn't have the political role that it used to have. The size of the public that appreciates poetry and is sustained by it is smaller, but their comprehension is very profound. This is an audience that reads a lot. The only censorship is commercial censorship—the most unforgiving of all!

"I had many chances to emigrate, but I just haven't had the desire to leave. You have to be really miserable to leave your homeland. Life in Russia is still bearable. My public is here; they know me; my language is and will remain Russian. In the U.S., I could fill ten auditoriums in a row, but what would happen after that?"

CHAPTER 17

Vassily Valerius is the son of the Soviet artist Yevgeny Viktorovich Vuchetich (1908–74), who sculpted the gigantic statues of Lenin found in public squares throughout the former Soviet Union.

"Valerius is the family name of my mother's first husband, who came from Belgium. He was arrested and shot in 1937. My mother, who was Jewish, then fled to Moscow to escape certain death. Just before the Great Patriotic War [World War II], she found work at the construction site of the Palace of Soviets, the unfinished dream of Comrade Stalin. Being an engineer and economist by training, she directed the interior-design teams for that building. She was one of the first women to pursue design in the USSR. At the time, we called it 'aesthetic technique.'

"When I was a kid, since our apartment faced the palace site, I observed its evolution. The first geologist's reports weren't accurate, and the foundation filled with water. Then the war broke out and the iron framework was used for armaments. After the war, that project was never restarted.

"That's where my mother met my father, a sculptor, in 1937. They got married in 1940. Even though she descended from a family of educated Jewish merchants, she was a committed

Communist. By the age of fourteen she believed in the Revolu-tion. My father was from Rostov-on-Don, and his father had worked as an engineer in a petroleum refinery in Chechnya. Much later, I learned that my father's grandfather had been a Yugoslav aristocrat, but that was a background it was best not to publicize at the end of the thirties. I never even heard his patronym spoken." [The customary and respectful form of address for a man in Russian is his first name along with his father's first name, with a suffix meaning "son of" attached to it, called a patronym.]

"In those days it was best to have neither roots nor per-sonal history. Today the opposite is true. Everyone searches for his roots. Every Russian is on a quest for his identity. That's why my mother lied. She told me that her father taught in a Jewish religious school when in fact he was a merchant. She claimed to come from a poor family of twelve children, but reality didn't conform to the image that my mother wanted, so she changed it. I think she believed it herself by the time she told me. She had forgotten reality.

"My father went to the front and returned as a captain, but wounded. He went to work in an art studio. His specialty was life-size portraits of field marshals and generals. He excelled in portraits in full-dress uniform, never making a mistake in the details, especially in the rows of medals, which was essential. Then he won a contest to build a monument to the victory of our troops in the liberation of Berlin. His concept, which Stalin loved, consisted of a sculpture of an immense soldier carrying a little girl in his arms. The idea of adding a child actually came from my mother.

"After winning this prize, my father started to earn a lot of money and could afford to build a house in Moscow. The street on which it sits carries his name to this day. That house belongs to his second wife now. I was ten years old when my parents divorced in 1953.

"When it came to art, my father was a pure naturalist. My mother thought that Russian art would move away from ideology and back toward other aesthetic criteria. My father lived in a more politicized environment and his art did not evolve. He was a simple man who had chosen to serve his homeland. They never stopped arguing. Moreover, my father, who adopted the lifestyle of a successful Russian businessman, had started to drink.

"In the end, they asked me who I wanted to live with. I chose my mother because I hardly knew my father. At that very moment, he was offered this apartment in the Stalinist vysotka on Ironmongers Quay. He moved into his own new house and gave this apartment to my mother. We moved here in 1953.

"My father never set foot in the vysotka, but he did come to my school once a year, on my birthday. He developed quite an act. He would arrive wearing a white uniform, looking very proud of himself, and tell me stories, particularly about the Second World War. He embarrassed me in front of everyone, disappeared until the following year. I didn't want to depend on him and always returned the pocket money he sent me each month. When I turned eighteen, he stopped contacting me. I never saw him again.

"I was admitted to the Institute of Fine Arts in 1962. I had applied a year earlier but not been accepted because of my father's name. We were in a state of 'thaw' then, and most of the teachers at the institute hated the work of the monument sculptor Vuchetich, and they were perfectly right. It was crap— mainly because it served the Soviet regime but also because it was bad art. However, if he had not lived under this regime, I think my father would have become an honest portrait painter, and his style would have been different. It's hard for me to pass judgment on my own father. To be sure, he was an uncultured man who knew nothing about art. He created the enormous *Statue to the Motherland* in Volgograd in 1962 and died in 1974 under the regime for which he had never stopped working, hav- ing covered the Soviet Union with monuments to the glory of Lenin. Lenin enriched my father for decades. He made him a millionaire.

"I've been ashamed of my father all my life, and devoted myself to doing the opposite of his work. In 1963, I won a contest to do the cover of a specialized newspaper called *Polygraphy*, edited by a man who had belonged to a group of Constructivist artists in the twenties and who detested the Soviet power. In fact, the whole thing ended pretty badly. I had envisioned an entirely black cover, both dull and glossy, which the editor didn't like. So the second prize winner's cover was selected. Mine was never even published.

"In 1968, when my first book was published, I decided to use the name 'Valerius.' I even retroactively changed my name on all my diplomas, which seems to have infinitely displeased my father. The day I went to the passport office in our building to apply for the change, the clerk had the nerve to call and notify him. In 1973, a year before his death, I wanted to renew contact with him but had no luck. He was always either travel- ing or sick. Actually, I think he just didn't want to see me again.

"I got divorced from my first wife and married Sveta in 1972. By then my mother had been living alone for five years on Ironmongers Quay. I knew it wouldn't have exactly been paradise to live with my wife and her, so when we returned we partitioned the apartment and created separate entrances. We lived that way for nine years, until my mother's death in 1986.

"The fact that this building is classified creates a whole array of administrative techniques to solicit bribes from owners renovating their apartments. The building's design doesn't correspond with its functionality. Some walls are very thick, others thin as cigarette paper. The architect, Chechulin, lived in an apartment downstairs, said to be the most comfortable in the whole building. But you can hear everything down there, which is a truly serious construction error! If I ever have to sell this apartment, I'll get a fortune for it, but only because there is a view of the Kremlin. . . .

"The early sixties were an interesting time. Though we didn't yet know it, the system had already started to fall apart. Things were loosening. Unfortunately, what happened in Prague in 1968 showed us the cruelty of the system once again. After the adoption of the new constitution under Brezhnev, I was summoned by the Party to ask me to work on a model for a limited-edition book cover to encase the constitution. I refused, which certainly didn't help my career.

"Then I got interested in theater. A friend who was an actor in Yuri Lubimov's troupe was going to put on a show in Krasnoyarsk, in Siberia. I wanted to decorate the scenery. I created other theater sets in Vladivostok and in Poland, and so on. I also designed the costumes."

Casts of ancient sculptures lord it over the shelves. Vassily Valerius shows me a sculpture made by his mother and then a photograph, torn but taped, showing a sculpture of his mother done by his father, who smashed it at the time of their divorce. This photo is all that remains of Valerius's father. He doesn't want anything else.

"For a long time I worked as artistic director for a publisher specializing in art books. Recently, the management made me understand that we had to appeal to the 'new Russians.' I walked out on them. I am not ready to compromise the quality of the work.

"The founder of this publishing house is a former professor of mathematics at a secondary school in the Moscow region. In 1991, as soon as the USSR dissolved, he started to paint watercolor landscapes on wet paper, a very simple technique. They were an immediate success, and he made a fortune in record time. Then he bought paper in huge quantities, when it was almost impossible to find, and began speculating. Within a few months, he had accumulated enough capital to start his publishing house.

"Of course, he had no idea how to run such an operation, but knew that it would pay off because at the time it took so long for anything to get published. Eventually he specialized in dictionaries and in the fall of 1999 he called me. I made his first book with the help of my daughter, who is both my colleague and my assistant. He quickly realized that I was good at it. He was also very proud to have me working for him, as I learned later. Still, we had financial disagreements. He didn't understand that a specialist costs more than a nonspecialist; in other words, that quality comes at a price. Publishing art books is a skill all its own, something my ex-employers didn't want to acknowledge. They were paper speculators only interested in profit.

"Working in publishing was much more profitable ten years ago. Today, the print media are losing ground to electronic publishing. What is happening to books is what happened to painting when photography arrived. Painting lost its practical side and became an art. Today, everywhere in the world, the cover of a book is more important than its soul, what's inside—books are turning into artistic objects and their design a subject of artistic research.

"I have the honor of being one of the six people to start book design in Russia. Before us, books were merely decorated—their design was purely functional. Unlike most others in this field, I think that book design is a true art form. At fifty-nine, I don't work anymore, except on special projects—like for example a book about celebrating the centenary of the Art Theater, in two volumes, or another on the seventy-fifth anniversary of the Meyerhold Theater. These aren't commercial projects. They aren't the kind of books sold in bookstores.

"Anybody here who has succeeded in his profession has thought about emigrating. It's too late for me now. At the time when I could have done it, I was afraid I wouldn't be able to overcome the language barrier, the change of lifestyle, in order to settle in Brighton Beach, New York.

"However, I'm not comfortable in Putin's society. And I think that things will get worse. At school, our system of grading goes from zero to five, three being the average. That's the situation in our country. We are a country of 'average students,' of whom President Putin is an example. At the KGB, he never even made it to become a general. He only went as far as lieutenant colonel. That says it all. The hardest thing to accept is that he pleases the Russian people. That's always how it goes. He has created a facade of solidity and of power, although in fact he is very weak.

"Lots of KGB professionals, probably the most intelligent ones, have quit to work in commercial companies where they are better paid. There's no one in the 'organs' except the rabble, which bodes poorly for the future. That's why I wish my daughter and her family would emigrate, but she seems to hesitate for the same reasons I do.

"Will things get better? Overnight they proclaimed the advent of capitalism and privatization. But it takes money to create all these new companies. Who has this money? Those who stole it. This phase of primitive accumulation has all been illicit and happened much faster than it would have in the U.S. or in Europe.

"Officially slavery in Russia ended only one hundred and forty years ago. That's only five generations! Attitudes, however, evolve very slowly. Moreover, a twisted form of slavery reappeared under Stalin, and today the way of life of the so-called 'new Russians' isn't so different from that of our ancestors. In a country where thirty to forty percent of the population is made up of the prisoners—whether political prisoner or common criminals—it is precisely the rules of the camps or the prisons that prevail, even in civilian life! That's why there are brutal hazings in our army, and that's why our language has incorporated so many *zek* terms. Even our police officers are to greater or lesser degrees involved with criminals. They divide the spoils with those whom they're supposed to be putting behind bars. The new mafia gangs are made up of these very police!

"No one knows what's going on in Putin's head. I get the sense he's using the fate of Russia to reach his personal goals. I didn't have the same feeling about Yeltsin. His last years in office made us ashamed, but he was a far more sympathetic man. I naively believed Putin wouldn't be elected, but I was wrong. It's a real catastrophe for our future—mine in particular and those of artists in general.

"Today, everything breaks down according to age. Everyone over seventy is nostalgic for the past. Everyone between fifty and sixty is disappointed and has a hard time adapting to the values of a society so disconnected from the paternalism, that of the czar or the Master. Everyone under forty has adapted one way or another. Last, everyone under twenty-five is the best off because they have never known anything else. It will be at least forty years before we see any improvement.

"I lost my all my socialist illusions long ago. Now I'm even more liberal than the SPS [pro-business party]. Everyone who was disappointed with the 'shock therapy' capitalism of the nineties voted for Putin in 2000. He embodied the hope of restoration—hopes on which he continues to play. The recent closing of the television channel TV6 didn't provoke any reaction from our citizens, but not because people agreed with what he did. It was because they knew action wouldn't do any good. Everyone retreats into his kitchen to talk about it, just like in the old days. Political jokes are back, too, which is a sign of a return to an era of great stagnation.

"The intellectuals keep quiet because they know it doesn't

do any good to speak out, that it's even become dangerous because there is no civil society. Here, speaking out has always meant risking your life. To express an opinion was a heroic act, which is not at all the case in the West. To use the well-known anecdote, Russia is a trolley car on which half the passengers are seated [a pun on "in prison"], while the other half tremble in fear. It is certainly not the first time that our intellectuals have held their tongues, but now they're helpless against the criminals—businessmen or oligarchs.

"Lenin's words come to mind. Intellectuals never agreed among themselves and never could organize themselves as a class. Great! And thousands of them have emigrated. Today there are more Russians than Jews in Israel. The politicians are all delighted with this, because now they have no further need for civil society. There is no longer any debate about anything. It is the reign of total inertia."

PART THREE

RENOVATIONS

CHAPTER 18

CENTRAL SECTION, FIFTEENTH FLOOR:
WING VK, FORMER TECHNICAL DEPARTMENT

CENTRAL SECTION, TWELFTH FLOOR:
THREE BUSINESSMEN

When businessmen—bachelors, for the most part—move into the vysotka, their highest priority is to remodel their apartment from top to bottom. Three of them—two Americans and a Russian—permitted me to enter their renovated interiors. Hardly anything remains of their apartments as originally conceived in the fifties. (Most of the vysotka's other occupants, however, have preserved the original ambience, either voluntarily or because they can't afford to do otherwise.) Not only have the ceilings been lowered, destroying the impressive aura of height and hiding the neoclassical moldings, but also most of the walls have been knocked down to open up the space. An air purifier has been installed in one of the apartments. Another has an imitation stained-glass window in the ceiling.

In contemporary Moscow, kingdom of the ephemeral and the superficial, traditional design tendencies may be dying, but design is still far from the minimalism of Japanese, American, or Italian architecture. In this megalopolis of 8 million inhabitants, where 70 percent of the financial resources of the country is concentrated, the housing market is constantly expanding and the subject of lively speculation.

"In Moscow," notes the architect Cherediego, "rich people want to live as close as possible to the centers of power. They no longer know where to invest their money, and the least risky place is still real estate. These people buy apartments for their second wife, their children, their uncle, their cousins, having already built themselves two or three cottages in the suburbs." The most expensive apartments, with a view of the Kremlin, are priced between $400 and $500 per square foot, which means that an average-sized two-bedroom apartment costs half a million dollars.

Richard Deates, a thirty-eight-year-old American financial manager, lives in a four-room on the fifteenth floor of the central sector.

"I arrived in Russia at the end of 1994, at the beginning of the first war in Chechnya, which was hardly the best time to do business. In April 1995, my partners and I created an investment fund called Renaissance Capital. At the time we were the only foreigners doing this. There was almost nobody else in the market. Our partnership lasted until the financial crisis in the summer of 1998, when we split up. Today, I am a specialist in debt reorganization. Moscow is my geographical base.

"I rented this apartment in 1995, moving in after one of my partners, who had occupied it for ten years, moved out. The owner, a widow named Tatyana Pavlova, refused to sell it. Her son had immigrated to the United States and she visited him there every six months. Periodically, I suggested to her that she should move close to him permanently, trying to convince her that selling her apartment would allow her to spend long and peaceful years over there. When the financial crisis hit, she still hadn't made up her mind. Finally, her son needed money to buy a house in Minnesota, so she agreed to sell me her apartment. The money from the sale even allowed her to buy another one in the building.

"Being in the banking business, I found the purchase negotiations were something hilarious. Tatyana Pavlova came to see me, accompanied by an alleged business adviser who tried to extort much more money from me than this space was worth. I was patient. They ended up coming down to my price, and in 2000 I bought the apartment for around two hundred thousand dollars. The renovation cost a lot more. I already had ideas about the interior decoration and about the quality of materials that we could use. My girlfriend, a Bulgarian who is studying at an American business school, helped me a lot. I had to hire a designer as well as a builder. I wanted to take full advantage of the space, get rid of this long corridor cutting through and one at the other entrance and enlarge the bathrooms."

The metamorphosis is surprising. The only remaining original element in Richard's apartment is the heavy double outer door made of teak. The ceiling in the foyer is covered with Indian fabrics embroidered with golden thread. The walls in the living room have been painted a pale yellow. The bedroom has been enlarged by the removal of a hallway, and one entire wall is covered with a panel of mirrors. What used to be a kitchen is now a small angled office with a bookcase. To the left, the living room opens onto the dining room, at the back of which is an elevated alcove in which sits a sofa. Sliding doors separate the stainless-steel kitchen from the rest of the apartment. In every room, music floats out of nowhere. The ceilings have been lowered to create space for an air purifier.

The windows looking out over the Yauza and Moscow River are triple-glazed. All the floors are Indonesian teak. An immense table and chairs made of wrought iron are from Morocco. On the wall are contemporary paintings bought in Bucharest. Extending the length of one wall of the living room is a console on which rests a large-screen TV, a Buddha surrounded by five monks, and some nineteenth-century Burmese sculptures. The wall tapestries were bought in Azerbaijan. Unlike most of the foreigners who come to Moscow, it seems clear that Richard Deates doesn't shop at the flea market at Izmailovo Park.

"I wasn't familiar with the procedure to get building permits, or with the degree of complexity and corruption in the bureaucracies. I am an expert on financial matters, a graduate of Yale, but Russia is still a mystery to me. I had to hire somebody to do all this for me. You have to go through dozens of departments—sanitation, fire safety, labor—all of which absolutely had to be bribed. We started in August 2000, and this process of getting permits wasn't finished until mid-December. When my agent showed me the final permit, everything seemed fine except for a 'period of validity,' which was only four months. 'A simple administrative detail,' he assured me. 'This expiration date is not important.'

"The problems started when we proceeded to the final step—getting agreement in writing from neighbors. The people downstairs signed without hesitation, but those above—an eighty-year-old retired general, his wife, and their daughter, a fifty-five-year-old pianist who breaks my eardrums with her scales and arpeggios every Saturday morning—refused to sign. That got things off to a bad start, though their consent to the work was ultimately only a formality, which we could do without.

"During my long business trips in the first half of 2001, I kept up with the progress of construction by E-mail. Then the upstairs neighbors reported us. They complained to the authorities. The police came and stopped the work and put the apartment under seal. The old general claimed that the renovation would cause the vysotka to collapse, taking him with it! He was convinced that once my walls (allegedly supporting his) were knocked down, the whole building would crumble! By calling on all his old contacts in the prosecutor general's office, he managed to get to the highest authorities in the city. The mayor, Yuri Luzhkov, passed his letter along to different departments for follow-up. As a result, all the authorizations I had obtained the previous fall were canceled under the pretext that the expiration date had passed. The fact that I am a foreigner, an American as well, didn't help me of course.

"I wondered if I'd have to start all over again from the ground up. It would never end. Exhausted by all of this, one Saturday afternoon I decided to go and meet my neighbors, the source of all these complications. I prepared myself so my anger wouldn't show, in spite of my exasperation. I had lived in Russia for five years; I had learned the language. For me, this visit was like my final exam.

"The general opened the door and let me in. His apartment was typical of Soviet interiors, where everything has piled up for decades. In spite of the chaos, I spotted right off some very beautiful nineteenth-century Russian fabrics. The two women were so surprised and panicked that after twice asking me if I wanted tea, they forgot to serve it. All four of us sat around the dining table.

"I spoke first, emphasizing how much I respected them,

trying to make them understand that during our five years as neighbors we had never had any problems. In his response, a tirade that went on for thirty minutes, the general admitted that indeed they did not have anything against me, that they knew that the apartment was my property and that I had the right to renovate in any style I chose, but he reiterated all his fears—that the work would destabilize the building. As it is, a skyscraper sometimes sways with the wind. The neighbors were afraid to step outside, fearing that the sculptures would fall on their head. 'It won't happen today or tomorrow, maybe not even before we die, but sooner or later the building will fall,' he kept repeating in a grave tone. The two women listened to him religiously, shaking their heads.

"I pointed out that my contractor, a building engineer, didn't share that opinion. I wish I hadn't said this. The two women started to howl that this pseudo-expert didn't know anything, that he had obviously bought his license, that in this country everything was up for sale.

"My primary goal was to get my neighbors to let me restart renovations, or at least let my workers install the windows. Playing their game to a certain extent, I scared them by pointing out the sight of missing windows indicated that the apartment was empty, and that this gave the wrong ideas to homeless people. I had to play on their insecurity. I wanted to force them to agree before I returned to the U.S. for the whole summer. They finally promised to let my workers put in the windows.

"My secretary called them on Monday morning—they had forgotten about their promise! My last weapon was to threaten them. I told them I'd use my contacts in the Moscow city administration. I told them that nothing would stop me, that I would see this renovation project through to its completion. Finally, after a four-month stoppage, work was restarted in August 2001 and I was able to move back in January 2002."

Henrick Winther is half Danish and half American but grew up in France. He came to Russia ten years ago, married a Russian woman, and is in the process of buying a fabulous space that takes up the entire top floor of Wing V, which he intends to turn into an apartment.

For the time being, the space in question, formerly office space in which the building maintenance staff lived from time to time, still doesn't resemble anything like an apartment. Old Russian technical manuals sit on the shelves. On the wall a 1998 calendar hangs next to a black-and-white signed photograph of the actress Ladynina (who lives in the building) and a subway map. The renovation promises to be formidable.

"When I finally decided to buy an apartment in October 2000, I contacted an agency, which soon drew my attention to a 'property of interest' that was not yet 'officially' on the market. It was a complicated situation, as is so often the case in Russia. I was hoping to find something with around three thousand square feet, so I asked to see it, and immediately fell in love with it. It consisted of two towers of two floors each, separated by a large terrace. Amazing! Altogether it consisted of seven thousand square feet—a bonanza! I immediately sensed the potential, though I already knew that it would be necessary to demolish it and rebuild it.

"I knew the vysotka on Ironmongers Quay because I'd been here to visit some expat friends. My real estate agent, who had good contacts at city hall and knew how the apartment bureaucracy worked, warned me that the red tape would take at least three months. It's been a year and a half, and will probably take until the end of this year!

"The problem is that the space I want to acquire has not been privatized. It is a former office that belongs to the city of Moscow and has never even been rented. In fact, there are two technical offices—the towers—connected by a roof terrace. Nobody can legally acquire a roof. But in Russia, anything is possible. Renamed a 'winter garden,' the terrace becomes salable. I've been a tenant there for a month, a sine qua non condition before being able to buy the space. Legally, I can only rent five hundred square feet, so each time we reregister a new sector of the space we modify my agreement. All that takes time, but when this process is finished, I will be able to privatize the entire unit.

"The city is apparently willing to sell, but everything drags on because of the novel nature of the transaction. The rent I'm paying, and then the purchase price, will enrich the city's coffers. And besides, I'm increasing livable space, since it had not been considered habitable. The official sale price per square foot is not that high, but since the surface area will be immense, the total cost will not be cheap. Particularly because the renovations will cost ten times the purchase price!

"Since the vysotka is classified, I don't have the right to change the exterior appearance of the building. From the street you'll notice two rows of columns on either side of the terrace, which I cannot touch, but from within they'll form a veranda. One of the two towers will be my room and the other will hold the kitchen. The staircases there now will disappear. I also want to add some windows, but that's another story. One thing for sure—there will be a swimming pool, a *banya* [Russian sauna], and a playroom. A project this big doesn't scare me. My parents bought a former police station near Nice at auction and turned it into a hotel. The reconstruction work was enormous.

"I came to Russia after reading an ad in the *International Herald Tribune* about a job managing a restaurant in Moscow. I'd never seen an ad like that concerning Russia. I was running my parents' hotel at the time. That ad struck me and I wanted to know more about it, so I sent off my résumé. They called me, then called back again. Finally I got an offer from one of the newest restaurant chains in the country, founded by a Russian émigré from Venezuela who had recently returned home.

"Back in 1991, there weren't any private restaurants in Moscow, so there was no competition. It seemed like a unique opportunity and I took it. I didn't speak a word of Russian and I knew nothing about the country. Our first restaurant was Le Chalet, followed by Patio Pizza, Santa Fe, American Bar and Grill, TGI Friday's, and lots of others. The nineties were really crazy. Our restaurants were the only ones in all of Moscow where you could eat for a reasonable price. People talked about us. Our dining rooms were always full. Today, our company has seventy-two restaurants throughout Russia, including in Siberia.

"I love adventure, and these last ten years have been the most marvelous of my life. We took enormous risks, which paid off. Today we have competition, but we were the first and still are. Our competitors are very stylish and very expensive. Their restaurants become chic for a while; then they're forgotten. Not ours. We put the accent on service. Our employees know that; more than the food or the drinks, they show our customers a good time. I treat my staff well by giving them promotions and bonuses. I need people who can smile and exude confidence."

Alexander Zeleransky is a fifty-year-old Russian who just moved into a two-room on the twelfth floor of the central sector.

"I was 20 years old in 1972, at the height of the Brezhnev 'stagnation.' Soon after I was born in Moscow, my parents moved to Saint Petersburg, where I studied languages. But I was not interested in becoming a translator. In the early eighties, I married a Frenchwoman and went to live in France, where I spent more than ten years. I sold fruits and vegetables in the suburbs of Paris; I was a taxi driver for a year—I know the city like the back of my hand. Then my wife and I tried to sell works by a Russian painter, in my opinion a genius of realistic figurative painting, but that didn't go too well. So I worked as a concert promoter in Russia. After perestroika, once I saw that the changes were for real, I finally returned to Russia, though I continue to return regularly to France, where I still have interests and where my ex-wife—we divorced in 1997—and my fourteen-year-old son live.

"This Stalinist skyscraper always fascinated me. This vysotka in particular looks like the wicked witch's castle in *The Wizard of Oz*. At night, you would think it was kitsch construction straight out of Disney World. There's one on Revolution Plaza, where some friends live. The arrangement of rooms isn't ideal, but all you'd have to do is knock down the partitions and renovate. I used to rent a great apartment near Patriarch's Pond. The windows looked out on the exact spot where the head of Berlioz rolls under the wheels of the trolley car in the beginning of Bulgakov's novel *The Master and Marguerita*. But Bulgakov fans liked to gather there and the place was noisy. Besides, the owners didn't want to sell. So I began to browse through real estate ads and ended up finding what I was looking for in this building. I know real estate well because my business involves buying land for the Anglo-American company British Petroleum so that they can put up gas stations.

"Like all crazy foreigners, I wanted an apartment with a view of the Kremlin. I bought on the third floor of the central sector, then exchanged it for one on the twelfth floor. I didn't want one higher than that. This vysotka has a pyramid shape, so the guy who traded his twelfth for my third gained himself fifty square feet plus a little extra money (under the table). But I got the view that I wanted.

"I had everything torn down, but not haphazardly. I hired a friend who was an army veteran to be the construction manager, and he got all the permits (administrative commissions, building architect, fire department, district sanitation services) without forking over practically any bribes—though I think he left behind some bottles of pretty good cognac! So we gutted everything except the load-bearing walls—between my bedroom and the living room—and hauled out hundreds of pounds of rubble. The work took twice as long as it should have, but this was my Russian interior architect's fault, the husband of a friend—a talented guy, but he drinks two weeks out of every month. He's the one who thought of the oval decoration on the ceiling for lighting, sliding doors, subdividing the bedroom into office and sleeping areas, glasswork on the ceiling, and the steps between the two rooms. He decided to lower the height of the ceiling. Construction took eight months. He also suggested that everything be painted all gray. The furniture is Italian. A friend got it for me. I refused to have a red carpet and curtains. I like the blinds better. More austere."

In fact, the apartment is entirely metallic gray, like a modern office. The outer door is equipped with a videophone. In the foyer, three long-stemmed flowers in glass vases add the only touch of color—along with the glass of red French wine my interlocutor is holding. The impressively large bathroom contains a Jacuzzi tub—with instructions in French and English—and a minisauna for one person. In the bedroom, which has an elevated bed, a stained-glass ceiling diffuses blue and white light.

"I have a large-screen television, so I don't go to the cinema. I'm content at home."

His portable phone begins to ring and he answers it.

"Incredible! A friend who's a traffic cop called me to ask whether he had returned my oyster knife! I recently taught him how to open oysters, because you can buy them here in Moscow now. They come directly from Rungis! A company will deliver them to your door. They cost a dollar per oyster, but they're fresh.

"Psychologically, it widened my horizon to live for a time in the West, but I think I'd rather make a career in Russia. Here, where history unrolls under your eyes, life is much richer in terms of personal and professional challenges than in the West. In the space of ten years, this once nightmarish and dreary capital of a Communist country has practically become a Western metropolis. I participated in the transformation by building gas stations. They're a notable improvement to the infrastructure.

We already have thirty-four, and three more are under construction. The first British Petroleum pump appeared one day in 1996. Since then, our competitors have been trying to catch up."

Photos of the vysotka are lined up along the windowsill.

"I hope that they'll tear down the Hotel Rossiya soon. My view would be much better. I'd look directly down on the Kremlin."

CHAPTER 19

Irene Commeau can work magic. From a scrap of cloth she can make a superb stole, a curtain, or a tablecloth, and she can just as easily transform a failing organization with no cachet into a select club whose members represent almost every Western business that has a Moscow office.

Ten years after buying a four-room apartment in the central section of the vysotka on Ironmongers Quay, she's still "not quite settled in," she likes to say with a mischievous air to her guests who are surprised when they see her apartment in such disorder. Open boxes are scattered around in the foyer. There are pictures, books, and knickknacks accumulated by her Russian family while they moved nomadically from country to country. The French side of her family (paternal), a recent heritage, is represented by a group of boxes filled mainly with old photographs.

On a wall of the entranceway, over a cabinet made of Karelian wood—according to Irene, "the wood of Karelia, that's Russia"—are framed photographs of the two branches of the family. They face us from opposite sides of an old mirror, as if to emphasize their mutual antagonism. To the left is the grandfather who "made it to Verdun" a few years after his marriage to Irene's grandmother. The couple poses stiffly for the photograph. On the right side are the Russo-Danish line: Great-grandfather Karl Kofod, a writer and agronomist who headed up the land reform project of Czar Nicholas II's minister of agriculture, who was assassinated in 1911; and Kofod's wife of seventeen years, Irene's great-grandmother, along with her entire class at the Smolny Institute, an exclusive school in Saint Petersburg founded for daughters of the aristocracy; it was closed in 1917. She is sitting in front of a painting of the emperor. Off to one side is their adolescent daughter, Irene's mother, in white sailor suit and cap.

"My mother was born in France of Russian parents who had left Moscow in 1919. Her family did not reject the USSR—on the contrary. In 1945, they cheered the victorious soldiers of the Red Army. Her childhood was spent in Italy during the summers and France and Switzerland in wintertime. Thanks to her Danish grandfather, her parents were not destitute immigrants. In 1953, she married my father, a French civil servant. She initially taught French, then Russian.

"At home we spoke Russian with our mother and grandmother. We also spoke Italian because my mother wanted her children to be trilingual like her. My grandmother had bought a house in an Italian village above San Remo where we spent long summers, and I am sure that my profound attachment to Russia comes from those summers when I followed the women to the stream where they chatted about this and that while beating their laundry. It's the environment you find in the *banyas* of Moscow, where women freely and endlessly tell one another their stories.

"We didn't go to French school, my brother, my sister, and

I, after the sixth grade. My mother had placed us in a Rudolf Steiner school where we did a lot of music and drawing, but when we returned home we opened the mathematics and geography textbooks from the Soviet school and the serious studies began. During the second trimester—from Christmas to Easter we lived with our grandmother—while we were little, we were passionate about winter sports, but in the evenings we had Russian studies to do, and during February vacations my mother came to see us and went over our homework. That terrified me. Morning: obligatory skiing. Afternoons: skate, eat, and study. We were bound to this regimen but also quite proud to speak three languages. Our use of time was strictly organized. On Sundays, my father took us to Catholic mass at the church in Saint-Germain-des-Pres. Thursdays, we went to the Orthodox church of the Patriarch of Moscow on Petel Road. Saturdays, a Russian woman came to teach us grammar and mathematics in Russian. She would tearfully tell me her personal history, how during the war the Germans invaded her village and sent the old folks into the church before setting it on fire. Throughout my childhood, people I was close to would burst into tears when they told me about their lives, and their woes were always related to the Soviet Union.

"My mother often took us to see the Soviet cinema at the club in L'Oiseau de feu [Firebird], one of the meeting points for Russian immigrants in Paris. There would be a mix of factory workers from Renault, old Cossacks, and all sorts of immigrants pining for Russia. When the Bolshoi Ballet came to Paris, we went to the opera house to see *Boris Godunov* or *The Queen of Spades*. I never saw a Mozart opera until I was an adult.

"My mother was a Russian professor, so I especially didn't want to become that. I loved the Beatles, read modern novels for teens in secret, and was horrified by everything the Soviet Union stood for. We didn't get an allowance, but I earned a penny per page for reading novels in Russian. Much later, when I met Igor Gaidar, I told him that I earned a lot of money for reading the complete works of his grandfather, who was the author of children's books that were much admired. I was really my mother's favorite guinea pig for this kind of experiment. Eating candy, was forbidden but I bought delicious chocolate rolls on the way out of school, thanks to my reading.

"My mother went to the USSR for the first time in her life in 1959. She could admire the Kremlin from the Hotel Bucarest every morning when she woke up. This trip was unforgettable for her because she got in touch with her roots and because the Soviet Union itself was so much more lively and charming than the French press had led her to believe. As far as she's concerned, everything that happens in Russia is good, whatever it is.

"I came to the USSR for the first time in 1964 with my mother and my brother, by train from Paris. Arriving at the Belorussia station was a gigantic shock. The entire platform was covered with people huddled over their bundles, sleeping. At daybreak, everything came alive. My brother and I went downstairs to the toilets, an immense room without doors, with people along the back wall in the process of taking care of their bodily functions. There was no traffic at all in the streets, but we were whistled at once when we tried to cross the boulevard without taking the pedestrian underpass.

"My mother took us to a *kommunalka,* the home of one of my grandmother's cousins. In the kitchen there were rows of gas burners. The pans were padlocked together. We also spent three enjoyable weeks at Yalta. Like the train station, the beach was a mosaic of bodies, almost naked. There seemed to be as many as the grains of sand. The local Intourist office helped my mother find a school principal who came to give us lessons and went with us on excursions.

"When I came back again in 1967, I was at the peak of adolescence and spent my time criticizing everything and singing in English. In 1969, my little sister and I went to a Pioneers camp deep in the heart of Belorussia. There were blueberries as far as the eye could see. I sat down in the underbrush and read for hours. I had already read Solzhenitsyn and seen the film *Andrei Rublev* by the banned filmmaker Tarkovsky. I was a source of illegal and valuable information to my school monitors and young friends. Our long conversations made me aware of all the misunderstandings between Russians and Europeans, but also about this new generation of Soviets' thirst for knowledge.

"A constant debate about the USSR raged within my family because my father, a senior official, had become more and more hostile toward the USSR, although he had liked it very much when he visited there in 1961. Things got particularly painful in May 1968, when my mother sympathized with the [Czech] revolt while my father was against it. My grandmother, a survivor of the Revolution and the famines, thought only about providing, as the family matriarch, for my mother, her daughter. Like all children, I wished that the adults that I was closest to were more understanding. Teenagers always think they know what's best for their parents, so I was busy explaining Russia to my father and France to my mother.

"I earned a degree in Russian in 1975 and got married while still a student two years later. I wanted to be a Sovietologist but had no idea what that meant exactly. At the time, there were no examples to follow. In 1980, my first job involved welcoming foreign figures at the Quay d'Orsay [French State Department], where my Russian language skills didn't do me any good because the Russians always had their own professional translators, as did the Americans, English, and the rest. So I ended up greeting the representatives from the Third World.

"A year later, I entered the Auguste Comte Institute, a wealthy think tank created by [former French president] Giscard d'Estaing. There I met Thierry de Montbrial [director of the French Institute for International Relations], to whom I confided that I wanted to become a Sovietologist. The following year I entered FIIR and was put in charge of all of the European Communist countries. I bought portraits of all the members of the Central Committee, I read *Pravda* every day, and I examined the order in which they were positioned in the photos. I crossed out those who had disappeared: Brezhnev, Andropov, Chernenko. There were more and more. All of a sudden, the USSR became interesting.

"When Gorbachev appeared, I went back to my mission in the Soviet Union. When I returned to Paris, bankers and businesspeople started inviting me to dinner to ask me about Russia. At practically every Parisian dinner party, people started talking about Russia.

"I joined the staff of Roger Fauroux, then French minister of commerce. I had met his daughter in the summer of 1989 while writing a book. I started to work as an adviser to the city

of Saint Petersburg, which was run at the time by the democratic mayor Anatoly Sobchak. Then I met Jacques Attali, special adviser to French president Mitterrand, then in the process
of setting up his European bank. He needed a specialist in the
politics of Eastern Europe and hired me to liase with the
Kremlin and other public authorities. The bank, the European
Bank for Reconstruction and Development, with headquarters
in London, quickly turned into a gigantic organization. Its staff
grew. This was the beginning of the age of cell phones and
E-mail. I worked nonstop.

"Then came the coup against Gorbachev. That evening in
his speech, President Mitterrand mentioned the junta and
called its members the 'new leaders' of the country. Mitterrand
was making a big mistake. He shouldn't have gone so far. I
immediately advised Attali to write to Gorbachev and Yeltsin
and offer support. I finally arrived back in Moscow at the
Hotel Metropol at the end of August 1991 with a suitcase full
of summer dresses. I needed to find offices for the bank, but
above all I needed to find interesting investments.

"I registered my son in a Russian school, but it was a catastrophe because he wasn't at the right level in either Russian or
math. The director of the school was assigned with bringing
him up to speed, for two thousand dollars per month, half of
the budget of the entire school! Thanks to me, the cafeteria
stayed open and the professors got paid. The first day of school
(September 1) went exactly according to the old tradition—
raising of the flag and a speech by the headmaster—but they
also celebrated the failure of the coup.

"I was looking for an apartment with a view over the Moscow
River and the Kremlin. I was delighted when they showed me

the eighth floor of the central sector of this building. I had never been in a Stalinist building. I found the entrance hall sensational. It was exactly what I wanted—a slightly luxurious setting in the center of Moscow.

"I immediately got started with renovations, which was a condition of the modest rent requested by the owner, the widow of an academic. I installed those beautiful Russian tiles in the bathroom. I wanted it to be both Russian and chic. For the curtains, I bought several yards of gray Syrian fabric—at the time, there was nothing better than that—in the GUM shopping mall and combined it with silks from Samarkand.

"After working for a few months out of a suite in the Hotel Metropol, I finally moved the EBRD office into a former COMECON building. The bank asked me to explore petroleum projects. One evening, I found myself in the anteroom of the minister of oil and energy, Vladimir Lopukhin. He was behind schedule, and it was past midnight. I was told he wouldn't be able to see me until the following Saturday. He was perfectly aware of the importance of the EBRD, and the fact that I came from the French Ministry of Commerce interested him. When I did see him, he asked me to become his adviser.

"And it didn't take long for the adviser to fall in love with the minister. I was determined to become a bridge between France and Russia. I helped Vladimir to understand the West, and I tried to better understand the new Russia, which I wanted to succeed. Vladimir was then at the peak of his career in a country with high hopes. It was the embodiment of perfection.

"He moved to Ironmongers Quay within a month. We decided to marry as soon as possible. May 23, 1992, the building's fortieth anniversary, I threw a magnificent party in my apartment on the eighth floor. I borrowed tables, which I arranged in a horseshoe in the big room and in the foyer. I covered them with twenty yards of fabric, this time pink and gray, also bought at GUM, and by the light of chandeliers that I borrowed from the antique dealer at the Metropol we nibbled on caviar and piroshkis. The guests represented the new class of Russian politicians: Igor Gaidar, who went on to become the prime minister; Anatoly Chubais, the 'father of privatization'; and several future oligarchs and captains of industry. Their bodyguards sat at a table on the landing. Seven days later, Vladimir was dismissed without warning or explanation. Some of those who attended our wedding reception must have known it was coming.

"In November, I bought the twelfth-floor apartment in which I currently live from Galia Yevtushenko. I liked Galia enormously with her bangs and blue eyes. I found her very 'Russian' and very self-confident. We negotiated for two months. I went upstairs to chat; she came downstairs for my cigarettes. She insisted that I keep the piano, a trophy of war, as well as a sort of monstrous cabinet that was custom-built for this space by the previous occupants and which can now be found in my country house.

"Galia had just privatized her apartment, but not everyone does. These days many people are wary because they're afraid— sometimes with good cause—that they won't be able to afford the monthly fees. Others don't see the advantage of becoming owners and are afraid of falling into a trap. Though privatization costs almost nothing, some little old ladies don't have any money at their disposal.

"I hired someone to get all the necessary permits to do the

work I planned. I started by replacing the electrical wiring, then the bathroom floors, the kitchen and toilets, for which I found tiles from Chelyabinsk—real Russian stone. On the other hand, I confess to having bought the faucets in Paris. Last, I repainted and varnished the floors.

"In December 1993 I had a son, then two years later a daughter. However, my relationship with my husband started to deteriorate. Our interests seemed to diverge. We are always searching, but for different things—me for Russia, he for Europe.

"In February 1994, as part of my quest for the real Russia, I bought some land and a run-down cottage about two hundred and twenty-five miles south of Moscow in the village of Petruchovo. A couple of ecologists had told me about this village at a dinner party. They had bought an old school there and converted it into their house. I went there for a visit during the summer. At the market in the neighboring town, about twenty miles away, I was struck by the abundance of products. I filled the trunk of my car with mushrooms, berries, and woven baskets. Petruchovo and the whole region enchanted me. The serenity contrasted with the horrors of Moscow.

"In the autumn of 1995, I bought another run-down cottage in the village, thinking that I would need a big house for the rainy or snowy days with my two children. Like my friends, I converted an old school into a home. The town used the money I paid for it to install gas service for the entire village. As had happened in the vysotka, renovation work in the country kept me plenty busy. Petruchovo brought me into close and regular contact with the real Russian culture. In a cottage we find the essence, whereas in a 'new Russian' apartment there is only the superficial.

"The work is almost finished. I now have a large house and two small ones over there, all equipped with heat and running water—a real luxury for a Russian village! I have furnished them by following the same principles I used here, re-covering old furniture from the neighbors and hiring local talent. The wooden tables made here are so beautiful. I also made a point of having large Russian stoves, the famous *pietchki*—just like the ones my grandmother told me about so many times in her stories.

"A new phase of my life began on December 1, 1999, when I began to run the European Business Club (EBC). It had been an empty shell of an organization, completely absent from the Moscow scene and unacquainted with the mysteries of the Russian power structure. It's up to me as to whether it becomes a valuable intermediary among the Western community in Russia. This is the sort of challenge I love; I fell back into what I know how to do. Today, the club's goal is to help Western businesses both better understand and act within the Russian context. At the same time, we give out the best information we can about Russia, whose image in the foreign press was—and still is—deplorable. I regularly invite sociologists, political scientists, and academics to talk about the country's evolution. Today, the club has become a very relevant organization.

"The current Russian regime is favorable to Europe because the Russian elites feel much more European than before. With the advent of the euro, which makes Europe much more stable, Russians are growing closer to the European Union. As Russia is such a large country, they understand that large units are better, especially since an expanding Europe is physically approaching their doorstep."

CHAPTER 20

Wearing a gray banker's suit, delicate rimless glasses, and slippers, Florian, who is German, invites me into his very modern interior, minimally furnished in the Ikea style. The Swedish superstore opened in Moscow in 2000 and has been mobbed ever since. His immense bookcase is only half-filled. During our conversation, he goes back and forth to it to look for files.

"After living for four years on another embankment, I was earning enough to pay a higher rent, and then, realizing that I would be staying in Russia much longer than I had planned, I decided to buy. From the architectural point of view, this vysotka seems to me the most successful of the seven. I wanted to live right in the center, and the idea of having a view directly on the Kremlin is attractive to all foreigners. I hope they never remove the red stars on top of each tower.

"A real estate agent showed me this four-room apartment on the ninth floor of the central sector. A family called Mikhailov lived here after their grandmother was given the apartment in 1952. The couple I dealt with was going through a divorce and wanted a quick sale. The woman, who was twenty years younger than her husband, had just left him for her tennis instructor. She was the more pleasant one. Her husband made it clear that I had better watch out because he was a salesman. Afterward, I invited them to come for tea in my new apartment, but they never came.

"In fact, they wanted to be paid in cash—as fast as possible—in order to start a whole chain of transactions and to buy two separate apartments. The deal was concluded quickly because the price was pretty low. This apartment was far less expensive than its equivalent in surface space (sixteen hundred square feet) would have been in the West. The Russians have so little confidence in their banking system that transactions are carried out in cash to avoid taxes.

"Moscow real estate is starting to approach European prices, but it's still very far from those of Paris or London. I would compare it with Berlin instead. The apartment and renovations totaled about two hundred and fifty thousand dollars. The BTI [Buro Tedhnitchesskovo Invenarizats] administration in charge of valuations is supposed to come up with a fair market price first. They estimated it as"—he goes over to the bookcase and searches through the files—"seven hundred and fourteen thousand, four hundred and sixty-one rubles and fifty-one kopecks," about twenty-three thousand dollars, "which is only a fraction of the price I actually paid. Selling at this price or higher makes the transaction taxable, which nobody wants, so everything is done in the dark and only by oral agreements.

"I didn't want to modify the apartment's internal structure. I liked the long corridors and the unusual placement of rooms. I even found a craftsman who restored all the doors to look like the originals. On the other hand, I did repaint, rewire the electricity, and upgrade the bathrooms.

"It is complicated and risky to become a property owner in Russia, because it's important to verify everything in advance to be sure it was officially privatized. In this case I discovered that the seller's underage daughter was still officially registered here even though she had been living in the United States for several months. I had to wait until she turned eighteen—luckily it was a matter of just a few months—to get her to sign a paper stating that she understood the terms of the real estate transaction and accepted them. If not, we would have had to appeal to a Committee of Minors, which would have necessitated even more time and money. So it was imperative that she come. Without coming out and actually saying so, her parents wanted me to pay for her ticket. I threatened to take back my deposit if they didn't bring their daughter back at their own expense. I had the time to wait, not them, so they capitulated. She came from Florida for only one day. Her parents took her to the notary; then she went right back.

"The operation of this building is unlike anything I've ever known. When I installed a second door in my outer entrance, they sent 'technicians' who 'recorded' it and verified that it met the 'standards!' The administration of the vysotka is divided into many committees directed by old all-powerful babushkas. In fact, corruption is the rule and each one acts as she sees fit. I'm sure the money that they soak me for 'elevator maintenance' is used for other things. You can see for yourself how the elevators were renovated!

"What is certain is that the majority of the elderly residents would be better off not complaining, because almost all of them have managed to own two apartments—one rented out for a high price (for cash) to foreigners and a second, smaller one, which they live in. The owner of an apartment downstairs put her four-room up for sale for five hundred thousand dollars while she lives quietly in a two-room in one of the wings. I would have bought it, but her price was too high. And then they whine endlessly about these 'miserable living conditions'!

"Here, as in the rest of Russia, the survival of the fittest prevails. Every time I went to see the chief engineer, I got whatever I wanted. I invested a lot in these walls, and now he knows that I would never for any reason let his technicians enter my apartment to bore holes in the wall to change radiators or ductwork. The tradesmen I hire will make an agreement with the engineer and will carry out the work properly.

"It's precisely because they didn't own anything that the Soviet version of 'ownership' was to accept everything that came from 'up above' without question. A few months after I moved in, an employee of the technical staff burst in one Saturday morning to 'examine' the garbage chute that my architect had closed off. Well, he reopened it! I called my architect, who advised me to never again open the door of my apartment to anyone from the building's technical staff. One of his workers came right away and blocked off the damned thing again!

"I do not share the opinion of those who think Russia under Putin is moving ahead. If some services are better—such as, recently, the facade of the building was restored; the main hall is clean—that's still by Russian standards. If you look behind the doors of the stairwells, it's horrible! Of course, the job of chief engineer of the building is meaningless now, but that's typical of the economy here—stuffed with ineffective and corrupt bureaucrats.

"My upstairs neighbor is a Russian banker who lives in London most of the time. There were water leaks in his apartment. Once again, the building technicians burst into my apartment, with the intention of boring holes in my walls to locate the leak. I screamed at them, especially since water, as far as I know, does not flow upward! They had already completely wrecked the tenth floor without finding anything.

"I have always been interested in history, and to me this building symbolizes the glorification of the USSR and Stalin. It was built by Italian and German prisoners of war, which terrifies me; I don't deny it."

In fact, the vysotka on Ironmongers Quay was not built by either Italian or German prisoners of war but by Soviet *zeks,* or political prisoners. This fact has been confirmed by Yuri Dykovitchny, one of its architects, but the myth about foreign POWs persists.

"I chose to live here because I love the architecture of the fifties and I have zero desire to pay three hundred dollars in monthly charges to live in a new building without soul, full of 'new Russians.' I would never buy an apartment in the House on the Quay, for example. It is too full of ghosts. This may not seem logical, because many people in this building also served the regime, but I think this building is so beautiful, particularly at night. I am in love with this building. The one on the other embankment looks horrible to me.

"I tried but failed to marry a Russian. I was very much in love. We had lived together for two years and our wedding date was set, but in the end I was forced to cancel it. She had already left me once before, then come back, which didn't seem very serious. It helped me learn the language, anyway.

"If the Wall had not fallen, I certainly would not be working here as the manager of an investment fund. It's a good illustration that this cynical, antisocial, and arrogant Russian society, where nobody pays attention either to the pensioners or to anyone else, has not, for all practical purposes, changed. After the war, Stalin stupidly ignored the ruins in Minsk and in Smolensk. He wanted his seven skyscrapers built in Moscow and he got them. Today, the state of affairs is the same—seventy-five percent of the investments are concentrated in Moscow and the other regions are ignored.

"Russia interests me because everything moves so rapidly and I can take part personally in the process, whereas in France and in Germany nothing budges. I don't want to spend my life in a country where I am constantly putting on the brakes. I feel freer here. I'm always telling the Russians that I am here for the long run. As a result, they have confidence in me. I've gained credibility, which you really need in my business, because I speak Russian. If I decided to go work in Paris for a year, who would trust me? But I have no illusions. I will always be an expatriate. At the same time, I feel very distant from the foreigners who only come here for two years, earn tons of money without paying taxes, and are not interested in the country itself.

"In the midnineties I made a choice, which I want to mention. Instead of relocating to New York, where my bank wanted to send me, I chose Russia, where nobody else wanted to go. I have not been disappointed. Not many others would have made this choice. Now, I am already a member of the board of directors of two Russian companies, a Saint Petersburg jewelry manufacturer and a Moscow bank. It would be psychologically difficult for me to go back to working in the West because I have more stature here. After having been a 'partner' at the age of twenty-seven, it is difficult to take a step backward. Admittedly, the competition is harder in the West, where positions are more desirable, but for those of us who survived the financial crisis of 1998 everything else seems easy. But it is not because I'm based in Moscow that I don't consider myself in competition with Western investors.

"Before moving to Moscow, I worked for a German investment bank in London. Today, I manage investments in Russia for the account of an Egyptian businessman. He had already earned an enormous amount of money before the financial crisis of 1998, and in 2001, a very good year, he recovered all his losses. We invest a lot in the petroleum industry, as much in listed companies as in firms not traded on the open stock market. Recently I was approached by people from the television channel NTV, and I took a look at their financial statements. I was horrified. You'd have to be crazy to invest in Russian media! Is there any newspaper making money in Russia? There aren't any. Why would a foreign investor put his money there?

"However, it is relatively easy to make money in Russia. During the last three years, investors were completely mistaken about their valuation of Russian assets. Those willing to stay in spite of big risks haven't regretted it. After the crisis, everyone thought that the Russian economy would be particularly bad, which was essentially the case. But as an investor you have to be interested in what is changing or emerging. In 1999, when I completely restructured our portfolios, I didn't ask myself if Russia had problems. Instead I asked if it had the capacity to overcome them. If you stuck it out, you were almost assured of making a profit, because few people will take so much risk. Russia is a place for adventurers, who are assured of a more than decent return on their investment. No way do I think that

France Telecom, Vivendi, and Alcatel are better and more certain investments than their counterparts in Russia! Today,
everyone is in the market. Russia has become fashionable. Of
course, my investor does not place the greatest portion of his
money here. Me, yes—but I live here. It's different. And the
amounts in play are also different. The longer I live in Russia,
the more I will want to take risks here.

"In ten years, the 'expats' in Moscow have become more
'Russian' and the Russians have opened themselves to foreigners. I have many friends related to my business, among them
more and more Russians, which was not the case a few years
ago. I spend my time crisscrossing the country to discover
interesting assets, whether these are the mines of Norilsk, in
the far north, the gold mines of Siberia, the far eastern port of
Vladivostok, the jewelry makers of Saint Petersburg, or the
large agricultural companies of Krasnodar in the south. When
it comes to agriculture, nothing is clear. The powers that be
make it unattractive to investors, and I am not even sure
they're doing it on purpose. It could just be the result of their
incompetence and their opposition to progress.

"In Europe, few people realize the proximity of Moscow, of
its power. The Russian capital is home to nearly ten million
inhabitants and it is very rich. I am optimistic about the future of
the country, which is not to say Moscow will soon rival Paris or
London, because the hardest part is yet to come. But Russia is no
longer at the edge of a cliff, like it was ten years ago. It is sitting
comfortably far from the edge, without really moving. Is this
because of Putin? In fact, the Russian government, as such,
doesn't exist. There are more than thirty ministers, a prime minister, and a 'shadow prime minister' who officially runs the presi-

dential administration. Of course, nobody ever agrees. The economic advisers have divergent views about everything. You never know what to expect from them.

"Putin is an example of the political consensus that started to form in the middle of 1999, when people realized that the uncontrolled capitalism that resulted in the pillage of the state could not continue. During the last years of Yeltsin, the state was very weak. All the Russian regions, including Chechnya, became as independent from Moscow as possible, and that ended with the bursting of the 'bubble' of financial speculation and the semicollapse of state institutions in August 1998. Entire industrial sectors were destroyed by market forces and theft on a large scale. However, since the crisis the state has regained control. Those who pulled off these sham privatizations realized that by continuing that sort of thing they would never be accepted by the Western world.

"The only criticism I have for the West is that it was not tough enough with the Russians during the 1998 crisis and still doesn't realize what is happening. I respect the fact that the oligarchs identified opportunities and seized them, but I don't respect their way of treating their employees or their business partners. You can think of them as thieves—you have to admit that they stole their startup capital—but you also have to recognize their capacity to survive! Berezovsky, Gusinsky, and Potanin are in fact very competent managers. However, to my taste, President Putin still has not distanced himself enough from them. Who financed his election? The oligarchs did; it's not a mystery to anyone. And so his margin to maneuver is limited."

CHAPTER 21

At half past noon, Willy Tokarev, wearing striped pajamas, opens the door of his apartment in Wing A, which was once used as a kindergarten for children of bureaucrats from the Ministry of the Interior and later became a communal apartment for the building maintenance staff. He carries his two-year-old daughter, Evelyn, in his beefy arms. Behind him, workmen are busily renovating the space, which is covered in dust.

The noise is so loud that it's hard to hear him, so we have to take refuge in the small studio at the back of the apartment. The room is cluttered with musical instruments, recording consoles, cassettes, compact discs, and concert posters, as well as an assortment of piano and computer keyboards. After asking his cook to prepare tea, he simultaneously gives orders to the workers, tries to appease his daughter, who is pulling him by the hand, and answers two cell phones, which never stop ringing.

Willy Tokarev, sixty-eight, is a small, square-shaped man. He sports an immense black mustache that hooks upward in two long, dramatic curls, and his dyed black hair is pulled back. The building guardians tell me that during the winter he likes to stroll around the vysotka's main lobby in a mink-lined coat while holding his daughter in his arms.

"My real first name is Vladilen, in honor of Vladimir Lenin, but I changed it to Willy. After school, at the age of twenty, I signed on with the commercial fleet. I wanted to be a navigator, but I ended up being a mechanic because of my bad eyesight. I adore the sea, and it was very exciting to visit foreign countries. Back then it was rare to have such freedom to travel.

"At each port of call, I went shopping for clothes. My first suit was French-made. I bought it in Istanbul. When I returned to my city after three years at sea, I had a habit of wearing a beret. Two days later, all the youths of the city were wearing them, sewn by their mothers. It had become fashionable.

"I was born in a Cossack village in the Krasnodar region [southern Russia]. When the Second World War broke out I was seven years old. My father left for the front, and the rest of the family immigrated to Dagestan, where my mother started working in a factory.

"I wrote my first lyrics at school. There were no musicians in my family, but my parents each had a good ear. On the shores of the Kuban River on Saturdays and Sundays they would pass the time singing and drinking with their friends.

"During one of my voyages by ship, I bought myself an accordion and learned how to play it. I started writing my own music. One day, I showed my pieces to a composer in Odessa and his face lit up. Obviously he liked them. He told me that I had a lot of talent and advised me to study music. From that moment on, I had only one obsession: to study at the Leningrad Musical Institute. Faced with my obstinacy, my parents gave in.

"When I arrived in Leningrad, I rented a room at an old

lady's house. As I was returning to my room one midwinter night, I passed an old man carrying a double bass down the street. He stopped every ten steps to rest, so I helped him carry his instrument up to his home. He was very afraid that I would damage it by dropping it. He turned out to be a musician from the Mariinsky Theater who lived on the ground floor of an old house. His wife kindly offered me sweet tea with bread, butter, and cheese, which smelled very strong. It was so good that I still remember it today. I told him that I wanted to be admitted to the musical institute. He himself was a graduate, and after noting that I had a good ear he offered to teach me to play the double bass. He was determined to inculcate me with musical theory. We worked at it two hours per day for two months. He taught me an elegy by Rubinstein, which I played for the entrance examination, and I passed."

Baby Evelyn toddles into her father's recording studio and starts to bang on the electric piano. She hurts our ears for a good ten minutes, but her father doesn't stop her.

"At the institute I met Anatoly Kroll, a well-known Soviet jazz musician. I had liked jazz since my days at sea. Kroll was surrounded by the best musicians of the day. I became bassist of his group, in parallel with my studies. We didn't play American jazz pieces openly, but our own compositions.

"A year and a half later, I passed a competitive exam to join the musical ensemble called 'Friendship,' where I started to sing tunes I had written. I spent my time touring and being well paid. Life was good. At the time—the early sixties—you had to have connections to be able to make records, so I didn't even think about it. I wrote for others—that satisfied me. I

earned so much money that I could even afford to eat toma-
toes in winter!

"It was at a Party celebration on November 7, the anniversary of the Revolution, that I found out my songs were not
totally accepted by the regime in power at that time. I had
composed a love song that did not mention the Party! It was
severely criticized. At that point I started to suffer from the
lack of artistic freedom and began to study the constitutions of
different countries to which I might immigrate.

"The KGB started to become really troublesome. When I
had a hit show with songs about sailors at the White Nights
restaurant in Murmansk [harbor city on the Barents Sea, north
of the Arctic Circle], the local KGB summoned me, suspicious
that I wanted to use the occasion to defect to Norway. They
made me follow them, which reinforced my intention to leave.

"However, I could have stayed. I had bought a cooperative
apartment in Leningrad; I was swamped with women and hon-
ors; I had so much money that I didn't know what to do with it.
But they didn't let me work as I wanted here. I never intended
to become a 'dissident' inside this country that I loved. Emi-
gration was a necessity. I chose the United States, which, for
me, symbolized total freedom.

"It was very hard to leave, psychologically and logistically.
Not being Jewish, I couldn't immigrate to Israel. I had to find
someplace else. It was the time when President Nixon came
to Moscow. The Party had let others leave before me, so they
finally had to acquiesce. In the course of our discussions, I was
careful not to say anything fundamentally bad against Russia,
because, indeed, I had nothing against my country. If that had

been the case, I would have been able to escape hundreds of times by water when I was a sailor. Others had done it. They didn't let me take out my bass, though. They thought I would never come back.

"Only I knew that I would return. I had promised myself. I only left to make music and a recording. My name was already known in the USSR, but I was ready to start again from scratch to build my audience and to compose freely. My parents also knew that I would return. However, my decision to emigrate destroyed the careers of my two sisters, who lost their jobs as soon as I left. I also was treated as a traitor in the local newspapers. Ten years later, however, when my records were successful, the KGB guys were anxious to get me to sign autographs!

"I arrived in New York from Rome, where I had stayed for twenty-seven days waiting for a visa. I had two hundred dollars in my pocket, lent by a friend. I rented a place on 176th Street from an Albanian emigrant and began to look for work and learn English. I wanted to adapt to the country as soon as possible, to be able to play by the rules.

"For four years I worked as a taxi driver. My first customer never stopped yelling at me, because I didn't know my way around the city and didn't understand anything he was telling me. Now I know Manhattan like the back of my hand.

"I had become a deliveryman for Ukrainian stores when I was asked if I would produce a benefit concert in Carnegie Hall for free. It was an opportunity not to be missed. I had one month to prepare myself to play the balalaika. I ran out to buy myself one in a novelty shop, and composed an arrangement of the song 'I Left My Heart in San Francisco' especially for the occasion. It was a huge success. A couple of Jewish Russian-American doctors came backstage to offer me assistance.

"For nine months I trained to be a nurse, and then went to work in the private clinic of these philanthropists. During my training period, I received ninety dollars per week, then two hundred and fifty dollars when I started to work. I was confused by such generosity! I accepted it, though. In 1978, I bought into subsidized municipal housing that had an extraordinary view of the Statue of Liberty. Three years later, I sold it because it turned out to be too noisy.

"At the clinic, I teamed up with a nurse who hated me because I was Soviet. She called me all kinds of names—including 'Communist,' of course. She was mean to the patients, too. One day, I gave water to an old man who asked for some, because she had refused to do it. I ended up complaining to the people who had hired me. They explained that they couldn't fire her because she was black and they could be accused of racism. But they did offer to lay me off so that I could qualify for unemployment benefits.

"Meanwhile, I had bought many instruments and had even started composing songs in English. I auditioned at Metro-Goldwyn-Mayer, where they found my music was 'old-fashioned.' One of the executives—a Czech—even advised me to write in Russian instead! But he opened my eyes. I hadn't realized that, in the evenings when I sang for my immigrant friends the songs that I had not been able to perform in the USSR, they liked them enormously. That's when I decided to record in Russian.

"From that moment on, my life became a dream. I had an insane success. For all the emigrants who had arrived en masse from the Soviet Union, my songs reminded them of their homeland. At first I was invited to play in restaurants for five hundred dollars per night. Then it rapidly increased to three thousand dollars. American students of the Russian language crowded into the restaurants where I was playing. In short, I had suddenly become so popular that in 1989 the Soviet authorities invited me back to the USSR.

"I was accompanied by a twenty-seven-piece orchestra, including the Kroll jazzmen, to give more than seventy concerts—a real triumph! Once, I even wrote a song about Gorbachev and his wife. It was very emotional to be able to perform songs for which I would have been thrown into prison fifteen years earlier. The authorities gave me a Russian passport.

"When I returned to the United States, I continued to perform in nightclubs and I bought a house on the seashore in Brighton Beach. I go back and tour in Russia every year. My audience is Russian, so I am bound to return to my country sooner or later. Today, I shuttle regularly between New York and Moscow. I own an apartment in each city.

"I met my wife Julia, a film school student, in 1994, in the Moscow subway. She was accompanied by her younger sister, who recognized me. I was lost, so I asked them for directions. Julia was nineteen years old. A month later, I invited her to one of my shows. I found her interesting and intelligent. We spent hours talking about politics and a bunch of other things. She constantly astonished me. We courted for three years before marrying. I wrote lyrics to her songs. Her father is an airline pilot in Magadan [far eastern Russia, where many gulags were located]."

Julia steps in at this point, having been introduced by her husband.

"In Magadan, I lived in one eight-by-ten-foot room with my parents and my sister for thirteen years. We had a grand piano because my sister and I studied at the music school. My father slept under the piano. When he left for work in the morning, he would always joke, 'I wonder if the one hundred and sixty passengers whom I am responsible for would believe that I just spent the night under a piano?'"

"Julia had lots of suitors, including one very rich businessman, whom she turned down for me. One night, leaving one of my concerts, our car passed by this Ironmongers Quay, and I confessed to her how fascinated I was by this vysotka. The driver then told me the history of its construction. It amazed me. Julia said, 'In one year, you will live in this vysotka, I am sure of it.' She's such an oracle.

"We started to look for an apartment after the birth of our daughter. We had gotten married secretly in 1999. Julia hoped my fame wouldn't embarrass her in her classes. We found this place in a newspaper ad. Because of my studio work, I needed a space without downstairs neighbors. We bought each room of this communal apartment from the four families who occupied them and relocated them, as required by law. I like living in a house in which I feel such strength and antiquity."

"When I arrived in Moscow at the age of seventeen to pursue my film studies," says Julia, "I rented a room not far from the Taganka metro station. When I walked through this neighborhood, pulling my heavy bag on casters, I looked like a real country girl. I often sent boxes of candy that I bought at the bakery on the corner of this vysotka to my mother and my sister. Then I'd go to the post office a few yards farther away. At the mezzanine level, which opens onto the courtyard, I would stop and look around furtively, but I never dared go inside. To cross this threshold was taboo; I could not get over it. Now I often take long walks in this same courtyard with my daughter."

"I'd like to continue to live between Russia and the United States," adds Willy. "Julia comes with me when I go to record in the States. She will probably get an internship in a film production company. She speaks very good English. As for my daughter, she will attend a Russian school from September to May and spend summers in the United States. I will do whatever it takes for her to remain a citizen of her country, Russia.

"There is mafia influence throughout show business, but in America you can always defend yourself against the phonies and recover your money. You feel more secure. In Russia, I've never received a penny for the sales of my twenty-six records, which are all bootlegs. I have complained to all the possible and imaginable authorities, in vain. These copies enhance my popularity but don't bring me anything. Everyone closes their eyes to this enormous traffic.

"Even as an immigrant in the United States, I always felt Russian. I couldn't forget my homeland. It's more than nostalgia—it's true love. However, I am not a nationalist. I feel sympathy for Vladimir Putin. I even voted for him. Nothing looks like it's improving, but I know what kind of person he is—a leader who will make major changes in life in Russia."

"A little after we met," says Julia, "Willy asked me to go live with him in the United States. I said no because I had to finish my studies. Besides, I wanted—and it's still true today—to live in Russia. He was touched to hear me say this, because after so many years as an immigrant, Willy wanted to return to his country. I remember my grandfather's reactions when there would be broadcasts about the émigrés on television. He wondered what they were missing in Russia. It makes sense that Willy would come back to his fatherland."

CHAPTER 22

Friday evening. When some Muscovites are getting ready to socialize, Elena goes back to work. She carries herself with ease, wearing a black tube top under a zippered Reebok sweatshirt. Her bleached blond hair falls to either side of her chubby, almost childish face. One lock of pinkish hair suggests a hint—misleading, as it turns out—of punk. Her nails are painted red. Elena drinks herbal tea and offers me water in a crystal glass. On the dining table is an assortment of roasted almonds that we will both nibble at during our chat.

Her two combined apartments were redone entirely by an interior designer. The former two-room opens onto the courtyard, while the three-room, which she recently acquired, has a gorgeous view of the Moscow River. Most of the walls have been removed, the corners rounded off, the parquet floors refinished. In Elena Andreeva's apartment, everything shines—the wooden table, the comfortable leather sofas, and the many mirrors. The corner kitchen is clean and functional. Painted landscapes on the walls depict lakes and forests. There is also one of a setting sun, extravagantly framed. The windows are draped with heavy curtains in Empire-style fabric. A flatscreen television takes pride of place in the middle of the living room. DVDs are stacked all around it, even on the floor. The exercise equipment looks incongruous on the thick carpet. The outer entrance door has been metal-plated and equipped with a videophone.

Energetic and ambitious, though also serene and realistic, Elena has built a well-regulated life. According to the weekly magazine *The News of Moscow,* she is number ten on a list of the fifty most prominent and influential businesswomen in Moscow.

"I moved into this vysotka seven years ago, after my divorce. When I was a student, I lived for a long time in a closet not far from this skyscraper. I always passed the Ironmongers Quay on the way to school and sometimes stopped to shop at the Gastronome, where all the stars of the vysotka did their own errands. I've dreamed of living here since then.

"My mother came from Omsk [Siberia] and my father from Nizhniy Novgorod [a city on the Volga River, northeast of Moscow]. They met in college and both became military doctors. They worked in Nizhniy Novgorod for a long time, in a science lab closed to the public. My father died when I was eight. His laboratory caught on fire. My mother moved to Moscow, and then we lived for a few years in Dushanbe, the capital of Tajikistan [Central Asian republic that became independent in 1991], where she worked as a physician in a subsidiary of a Moscow institute. At the time, eighty percent of the city's inhabitants were Russian.

"I wanted to become a doctor, too, but my mother discouraged me. She wanted me to distance myself from that male-dominated world, which had killed my father. I sewed and sketched very well, so I was accepted at the Institute of Light

Industry in Moscow. Today it's called the Institute of Design and Technology. To my mother's great despair, the business I'm in is, on the whole, just as masculine as medicine.

"Today I teach clothing design at the same institute. For my thesis, I invented a new technique for manufacturing and handling textiles much more rapidly. I had to create a production model to earn my diploma. Nothing in the USSR was ever done on a small scale, so I had to start with a production run of five thousand units! I had the right to sell all of it, and these were my first steps in the world of business. It was the beginning of perestroika, which gave me the chance and the taste for working for myself. I not only sold out my entire first production run, I made a profit.

"At the time, this kind of thing was not yet called 'doing business.' It was called 'fieldwork in defense of a thesis.' Still, I soon started my own company. I was offered a job in Belgium, but I turned it down. I wanted to stay in the USSR. I patiently pursued two lines—knitwear and furs. There might not have been anything for sale in Russia in 1991–92, but I was very busy with this new business. The command economy was giving way to contracts tied directly to commercial trading partners.

"While my business was getting better and better, the KGB was being reformed, and thousands of civil servants from the so-called 'organs,' in spite of their training, their deep patriotism, and their seniority within the organization, found themselves out of work. These men were experts in the courts as well as in the handling of weapons, but they were completely ill suited to adapt to new ways of doing business. Some of them offered themselves as bodyguards since I transported valuable furs. I knew that senior members of the state organs, able to handle firearms and ultradisciplined, would make the best security guards.

"I liked the idea of hiring them. The only thing we needed was the authorization to carry weapons. Under the terms of the law in force at the time, this kind of license, valid for three years, could be obtained for six hundred dollars. I spent almost all of my profits from two years in the textile industry to buy these permits.

"At first I used them [these guards] for my own protection, but then I told myself that given so many commercial banks were starting up, it made sense to offer my services to them. At that time, everyone needed protection. Little by little, this became my new business—particularly since, beginning in 1994, the textile industry had to compete with 'shuttles': travelers who went to Turkey or China and brought back their shoddy merchandise to sell in Moscow. My textiles became less and less competitive. It was time to move on to something else.

"I officially created the Bastion Security Agency on January 1, 1993. Today, I am the head of a holding company of six enterprises and employ a thousand people. We are one of the ten biggest security companies in Russia. I was the first in Russia to occupy this 'niche,' where the demand was enormous. Our clientele is from across the board.

"But the market evolves and we constantly have to adapt to it. Before the financial crisis of 1998, we were in charge of security for a number of small businesses, banks, and commercial spaces rented by people who were in the process of learning their trade. We also offered protection from murders-for-hire and kidnappings. This is no longer the case today. Our biggest clients now are business centers and supermarkets.

"The types of criminal behavior have changed considerably since 1991. During the USSR days, there were mostly classic crimes and car thefts by young juveniles. The early nineties produced a boom in large-scale racketeering. That's when we started to protect clients from organized crime within our police force. Finally—and luckily—the legislature has changed the penal code to include financial crime. Now, the racketeers have almost disappeared, mostly thanks to Article 163 of the code relating to extortion.

"However, attitudes haven't evolved as fast, and to some the idea of getting rid of a problem by killing someone is still tempting. There's been a slight change since Putin came to power. The organized crime members who once found protection in the halls of power and who used their contacts to get themselves elected are behind bars. Many criminal networks have been dismantled. There are fewer and fewer gangs. When I'm invited to appear on television, I always tell the audience not to give in to the crooks, that they should never pay them. Those who pay contribute to this scourge.

"Gone are the days when, for example, a liquor warehouse that was getting five visits a day from gangs claiming to offer them protection would call upon our services. We would tell these lowlifes that they'd better leave the place alone, because we were the ones in charge of security. Getting ourselves established was not easy. The quality of our service and our close attention to legality set us apart. Most serious businessmen realize we are worth more than the unknown companies, even though our prices are higher. But they are willing to pay us because our employees are honest and have Moscow residence permits.

"In the West, there are fewer police officers and security guards, because they've been replaced by surveillance cameras. Here, security is still manual labor, which is still less expensive. There is a lot of theft in Russia, maybe more than elsewhere. Russians don't understand private property. From gasoline to computer equipment—you have to watch everything.

"I don't know where Russia is going, particularly because I'm one of those people who do well under any political regime. As a student, I made good grades. Then I joined the Communist Party because I wanted a smooth career path. Then I defended my thesis and no doubt would have enjoyed the privileges of the old regime, but the wind changed and I adapted. I always found a way to fit in. During the Soviet period, my salary was well above average, and that is still true today. I lived half of my life during the Soviet era, the other half in post-Soviet Russia, and I am doing as well in the one as in the other.

"Yes, it's certainly difficult to work 'by the rules' every day, but that's what I try to inculcate into my employees. I am a businesswoman who specializes in the legalities of security matters. I am passionate about the technicalities of legal protection.

"The other day, my sixteen-year-old son told me that he had been threatened by a gang of bullies from his school who wanted to fight him. He didn't know what to do: turn his back and be called a coward, or 'go at it' and get beaten up? I told him that the law was on his side, because if a pupil got beaten up within school grounds those responsible would get kicked out. I made him understand that he was responsible for his actions. He followed my advice, and in the end nothing happened. The bullies sensed his determination. I am confronted with similar situations every day. The only way to deal with these people is to show them you are on the side of the law.

"Today, we concentrate more on legal consulting for Western firms that we protect against all sorts of risks. The subject of my thesis in judicial sciences was 'Criminality and Jurisprudence.' Now that the Soviet system has been dismantled, the old so-called 'tribunals of comrades' [people's courts] don't exist anymore, neither in business nor elsewhere. The days when everyone knew everything about the private life of their neighbors are over. Today, we don't know who lives where, no one is registered with the police, salaries are paid in envelopes to avoid taxes, and so on. The system of risk prevention has disappeared.

"More than a million prisoners are packed into our prisons. That's more than there were at the end of the Soviet period, not because the police are more efficient, but because more people are being thrown into prison. We don't have to return to the old system, but we do need to invent a new one. That's exactly what I'm trying to do at Bastion. But I wish the state realized the gravity of the problem and helped us to solve it. It's urgent that we create new processes before the arrest and the discovery of the offense. Predict crime to prevent it—that could be my political creed. That's the kind of debate I want to stir up if I get into politics. I'd use the experience I've acquired at Bastion, which is almost an anticorruption organization, to design a more complete methodology.

"My company pays the security guard you saw downstairs in our entryway, but he guards the entrance of the entire building.

When I moved here, I soon realized that most people couldn't pay for security but also knew that it was important to maintain order. So a few months ago I gathered together all the residents of this entry in the stairwell to discuss sharing the cost for the intercom [twenty or thirty rubles, about one dollar, per apartment], as well as other charges. Some penniless retirees asked me if I would pay their share. I didn't see why not, since it was well within my means. Besides, I took advantage of this to improve the stairwell and interior of the elevator."

Elena Andreeva's elevator is one of the few in the building to be equipped with a mirror, and the steps leading up to it are marble.

"I thought we should have a security guard after [the apartments of] two friends in the building were burglarized. Our guard watches my floor in particular, with the aid of two cameras positioned on my landing and two others facing the courtyard. My neighbors provide us with a list of their visitors. These measures, which might seem drastic, were taken two years ago, after the bombings in the fall of 1999. The residents of this entryway are so satisfied that some of them gave the security guard a small television and a table. He sometimes gets flowers. When I first moved here in 1995, a bodyguard used to accompany me up to the door of my apartment. After it was clear the threat was gone, I dropped the bodyguard.

"Under the Soviet regime, people elected 'district councillors' who were in charge of matters relating to residential buildings and social activities within their district. Most were retirees from the Communist Party. All this ended with perestroika. The state subsidies had dried up; the common areas were neglected, little by little. However, it would only take a minimum of coordination for the vysotka's administration to rent certain commercial spaces at high rates and use the money for renovation. But nothing has been done. All the commercial potential has already been exhausted and the residents of the building can't put together enough money to carry out the work.

"Because it's still managed by the municipality, this vysotka receives some subsidies for its community services. The occupants don't pay all of these charges. However, in Moscow's new residential buildings in the capital, the monthly fees can be as high as two thousand dollars per month. If everyone here paid a hundred percent of their share of the charges, they would quickly rise to five hundred dollars, which is unthinkable. If, as some would like, the building became a condominium, we would immediately lose these subsidies and the charges would still go up. I specifically bought these two apartments, in a municipal building, because the atmosphere is special here. Nobody comes here to talk business. The state is still responsible for maintenance of all common areas, cold and hot water, electricity, cutting the grass in the garden, and so forth.

"I am against those who want to turn our building into a condominium, simply because I refuse for my home to become a profit-making enterprise. If the building were to be completely privatized, we'd first have to figure out how much it would cost the residents. This pro-condominium group has already illegally registered itself as an association of co-owners. Their organization openly arrogated the right to come to a credit arrangement with any firm on our behalf. And if, for example, they were not capable of repaying their loan, who would do it in their place? There would only be two possibilities: sell the building or assess money from everyone. I am categorically against strangers acting in our name and indulging in commercial activities in our vysotka.

"The assembly of residents of this building voted against the condominium a few years ago. I hadn't really understood that a dozen or so people leading this pro-condo movement could be so indifferent to the destiny of hundreds of souls who would be obliged to move if the status of this building was changed. What inhumanity!

"I was called as a witness and delegate for my entryway in court. I purposely arrived in the latest model Mercedes 600, driven by my chauffeur, and wrapped in a very expensive fur coat, just to show that it wasn't only poor little old ladies nostalgic for the Communist system who were against the privatizing of the building. It was clear that anyone able to buy a one-hundred-and-twenty-five-thousand-dollar car could afford higher monthly fees. We won the lawsuit and their association was dismantled. For the moment, the matter seems to be settled. As long as Sofia Perovskaya [president of the Owners' Association] is alive, that's how it will be. And so much the better.

"I live alone with my son, and I am very concerned about protecting him. I have installed alarms inside the apartment," there are discrete switches along the length of the walls, "many of which are connected directly with the district police station. Each 'button' costs fifty rubles [$1.50] per month. If I press one, the police are supposed to arrive in five to seven minutes. I also have a portable alarm that I take with me when I walk the dog.

"As far as the education of my son goes, I have got things under control. He has two governesses, one to make sure he

eats right, the other to help him with his homework. Then he
has an English tutor, so his accent is very good. In my business,
I meet lots of children of the nouveaux riches, and I don't want
my son to become like them—badly behaved and spoiled. His
education borrows from both the best Russian schools and the
best Western educational systems. I don't want him to spend
many years in the West, where he would probably get married
and drift away [from me]. In Russia, we live as if on a volcano,
unsure of anything from day to day, but I still hope that my son
will remain close to my way of thinking, that he stays a Russian. It's a little egotistical, I know. I want us to read the same
books and talk over the same problems. I want him to be one
of Russia's future decision makers.

"In the same way that Rosbank"—one of Russia's biggest
state-owned banks—"is run by men who studied at the Academy
of Finance, like Vladimir Potanin and his friends, the group
around the economist Gaidar all came from the economics
department at Moscow State University. You see the same thing
today in Putin's entourage. They all came from Saint Petersburg
and knew him. That's a resource you have to know how to use.
But if my son disappears into one of the Western universities, he
won't go to his [Russian] friends' birthday parties and won't
become part of any group. He may turn into an excellent professional, but he would miss out on the most important thing—
being part of a network!

"But so that he'll also gain a Western outlook I send him
every winter to a school near Geneva—I take advantage of this
to go relax at the Grand Hotel in Montreux—and in the summer either to England or to German-speaking Switzerland,
where he studies languages, plays golf, goes horseback riding

and swimming. We'll see what he wants to be later on—banker or accountant. He's got lots of choice.

"His father, whom he sees every weekend since our divorce, has no say in this because I'm the one who finances everything, but he knows I'm doing the right thing. He earns much less than me and is in no position to clothe his son or buy shoes, either. An Armani suit may cost six hundred dollars, but I can afford it because I have only one son.

"I spend all my vacations abroad. I have been to the United States—to Las Vegas for an exposition about casino security. I've also been to Israel, Egypt, Greece, and Cyprus. I took my son along rafting in Bali, and on a cruise to France and Italy. For my birthday, I spend a few days relaxing at the Hotel de Paris in Monte Carlo. A table is reserved for me at the Louis XV restaurant. I often shuttle between Nice and Cannes in a rented Porsche to go dancing at Jimmy's. This is the kind of thing I would not have been able to enjoy twenty years ago. I returned from the carnival in Rio de Janeiro with a young friend three days ago. Last year I went to the carnival in Venice.

"This is what this new life offers me—in my career as well as in my vacations—the chance to do whatever I want, whenever I want."

CONCLUSION

With time, attitudes toward the vysotka on Ironmongers Quay have changed. A popular Moscow daily newspaper—*Moskovsky Komsomolets*—recently published the following about it: "It recalls the miserable epoch of Stalin and it always will. Let them do whatever they want with this building!" In the same article, however, one can also detect traces of an affection tinged with melancholy:

> Don't worry, dear friends, soon the "giant" will be unrecognizable. The old-timers who live there are dying off, and the traditions they preserve are disappearing with them. Will the building itself be able to withstand? Nobody knows the structural effects of all the modifications and transformations carried out by the new tenants—done without the slightest cooperation with the architects. However, you have to admit, if you close your eyes and imagine the Ironmongers Quay without this vysotka, is it still Moscow?

Since the advent of perestroika under Mikhail Gorbachev and the attendant privatization of apartment-building complexes in Moscow, the general aura surrounding the "giant" on

Ironmongers Quay has turned somber. Gone is the privileged status of the vysotka and its occupants. Some apartments have been resold as office space. Ceilings and walls have been demolished, staircases and lofts added. It seems somehow unacceptable that this structure should decline in prestige, that it has not undergone the repairs that would keep its past splendor from deteriorating inexorably.

Moscow City Hall has let the Stalinist skyscrapers crumble, but in his own way, the all-powerful current mayor, Yuri Luzhkov, loves their style. He is, he says, building a "new city." But this "new city" looks eerily like the old one. In 2000, using a new urban blueprint, he launched a program to construct sixty skyscrapers inspired by the seven Stalinist towers. According to this plan, a "new ring" of skyscrapers of thirty-five to forty stories was to be constructed over a period of fifteen years to replace, gradually, the five-story housing units built under Khrushchev in the sixties.

In the northern sector of Moscow, the Triumph Palace has already risen, a fortresslike structure with forty floors in its central section crowned with a spire. Originally, Stalin's architect had planned to build eight vysotkas, but the eighth, which was to occupy the place currently occupied by the Rossya Hotel, never got off the ground. Rumor has it that the building would have been taller than the Kremlin and that this was considered "awkward." Might the Triumph be the eighth skyscraper the Communist dictator never built? Dom-Stroy, a privately owned real estate developer, broke ground at the work site in the fall of 2001: it intends to use the renown of the other seven vysotkas to sell its own. Nine hundred apartments have already been sold here at a minimum price of $150 per square foot.

The promotional campaign unabashedly evokes Stalin and the "glorious years of his reign." In one radio spot, the Young Pioneers proclaim with joyous singing that they want to save money so they can buy an apartment in this eighth "giant."

Dom-Stroy is to have the endorsement of Mayor Luzhkov, to advertise its buildings. The developer has hit upon a formula that is both reassuring and enticing: these are "special destination homes" (in Russian, *Doma Osobovo Naznatchenia*) just like those the state used to have. In the press are ads comparing the Triumph to the seven skyscrapers in terms of prestige and solid construction.

The philosophy behind these new skyscrapers is that of a "city within a city," an enclosed world in which every retail outlet or restaurant is intended for the exclusive use of the building's residents and their guests, all contained within an environment that protects them from the dangers of city life. The Triumph would essentially constitute its own district, but "unlike an ordinary district, it will be inhabited by people who all belong to the same social level."

And what about the unfinished Palace of Soviets, inspiration for all the vysotkas, that languished as a flooded foundation after Stalin's death? In 2000, the Cathedral of Christ Savior was reconstructed on that site, where it had stood for centuries until Stalin had it torn down. It is now one of the most visited sites in Moscow, by tourists and locals.

I have let the inhabitants of the vysotka on Ironmongers Quay speak in this book. They've expressed their love for this building and their country, though for some this love has long had its paradoxes and ambiguities. They've told stories about their lives and shared their difficulties adapting to a way of life that was imposed on them with some brutality. These inhabitants are no longer the handpicked elite of yesteryear, but they are privileged all the same to live in the richest city in Russia. Clear-eyed, sometimes cynical, they reflect their country, stranded between the former Soviet system, still weighing heavily upon them, and the indefinable and fluctuating post-Communist world that the West has much trouble understanding. The condition has produced a multiplicity of misfits. And those who despise change on principle are no fewer.

Putin's Russia remains a giant in search of its identity. From a totalitarian economy the system has been radically transformed, assuming—much too quickly—the features of unrestrained capitalism. The "civil society" that has been so eagerly anticipated has barely emerged, and today's Russians—some awkwardly, others with greater self-assurance—would like their voices heard.

ACKNOWLEDGMENTS

Thanks, first of all, to Frances Forte, a loyal and generous friend who for many years has listened to and advised me with great wisdom. Her work with this project displays her innate talent for translation and her firsthand and deep understanding of how Americans see Russia.

To Tim Bent, my editor, who was the first to envision this book in English and who made sure it would meet the highest editorial standards. I have boundless gratitude for his handling of all those difficulties inherent in publishing a book on both sides of the Atlantic.

To Professor Donald Fanger, who has known me since I was a little girl and whom I knew I could count on, even at the last minute, for expert literary translation.

To my parents, Lucille and George Nivat, particularly my mother for her careful review and translations—in short, for all her invaluable help during the editing of the book in French.

In Paris—to my loyal editor, Claude Durand, who was the first person to encourage me in what I wanted to do. I'm equally grateful to Helene Guillaume, Martine Bertea, and the whole Fayard team for their confidence in me. Olivier Allais gave me the original idea. Philippe Deneux provides constant encouragement.

In Moscow—to Marina V. Chestnykh of the Russian State Library, Department of Special Files, without whom I would never have found the original texts by Gorky and Mayakovsky about the American skyscrapers. Marina loves her work and does it with a professionalism and passion for which I have great respect. I am also grateful to Yuri Rashkin, Anayt Oganessian, Sergey Krivonoss, Dimitry Savelev, and Sergey Riabokobylko.

In Capri—to Dora Iannuzzi and the personnel at the bank for their technical support.